GOT FRUIT?

WHAT IS YOUR LIFE PRODUCING?

By Rob & Lisa Laizure

FIVE STAR
PRESS

PREFACE

One afternoon we were sitting on our back patio when our youngest son came up to us with a tangerine. We asked him where he got it and he said it was from the tree by our bedroom. We looked at each other in amazement wondering how we never knew we had a tangerine tree! Until this tree produced fruit, we didn't know what it was!

Have you ever looked at a fruit tree and wondered why it has so much fruit? Have you ever seen a fruit tree with withered leaves and barren of fruit? Did you ever wonder why? What would cause one tree in an orchard to be filled with beautiful, good-tasting fruit, but another tree in the same orchard to be a dead tree with withered branches and no fruit at all? Why?

The same would be true in our Christian life. Why do some people seem to bear so much "fruit" in their lives and others don't? Better yet, what exactly does fruit mean in the Bible? Jesus seemed to talk at length about seeds, and fruit, and trees, a fact which might mean as Christians we should probably find out why it was so important to Him! Is it possible to bear fruit and yet the fruit you bear isn't real? What would it take to bear fruit that honors God? What are the criteria that Jesus calls for in a true fruit bearer?

That is what "Got Fruit" is all about. Sitting in a Bible study one day I was asked what exactly did it mean to have fruit. Are we all to have it? What does that have to do with our daily walk with Christ? Hopefully, this book will answer all these questions and more. Once again we will begin with the most important verse we will ever face, 2 Corinthians 13:5, which says:

"Examine yourselves as to whether you are in the faith. Test yourselves. Do you not know yourselves, that Jesus Christ is in you?—unless indeed you are disqualified."

Our hope and prayer for this book is that we examine ourselves, first to make sure we are truly Christians, and then to examine ourselves to make sure we are producing *true fruit.* Not pretend, plastic fruit, but *true fruit* that comes from knowing Jesus. As we study this topic together, may our lives be forever changed as we attach ourselves to the One True Vine – Jesus.

Our prayer is that our world around us will change because our lives will be changed. As you read this book, there will be many verses that will be repeated throughout the different chapters. We feel the more we see and hear these verses they will become a part of us. Hopefully at the end of this book we can honestly ask ourselves, do we "Got Fruit?" And hopefully the answer will be a resounding "Yes!"

TABLE OF CONTENTS

CHAPTER 1

ARE YOU ATTACHED TO THE WRONG TREE?

This chapter is by far the most difficult for us to write, not because we don't believe it is true, but because many people we know might be offended. Our intention is not to offend anyone. We have one goal in mind for this chapter, which is to show you that you might be attached to a certain church, religion, tradition, or way of life you believe is the right way to God, but could be unbiblical. This first chapter is written in hope and prayer that if this is, in fact, true, God will open your eyes to see you might be putting your eternal life in the hands of a "wrong tree."

Maybe you were raised in a certain religion, and you have been convinced what you believe is true. You go to church, you feed the homeless, and you help out your fellow brothers in the church. You are a nice person, your church is a comforting place to be, and besides, your mom and dad raised you this way. How could they be wrong? How could a church that is so big in the world be wrong? How could a church that is growing in numbers be wrong? How could my pastor, minister, priest or bishop be wrong? Let's see what the Bible says.

First of all, the Bible is very clear that everything written in it are the inspired words of God. Anything written outside of the Bible are not the inspired words of God. He only makes claims to the authorship of what is in the Bible.

2 Timothy 3:16-17:

"All Scripture is inspired by God and profitable for teaching, for reproof, for correction, for training in righteousness; so that the man of God may be adequate, equipped for every good work."

Proverbs 30:6:

"Do not add to His words or He will reprove you, and you will be proved a liar."

All Scripture in the Bible is inspired by God, or in other words, "God-breathed." He inspired 40 writers over 2000 years to put down the history of mankind, how sin has infected this world, and how man is separated from God because of this sin. The Old Testament points toward a day when there would come a Savior who would take away these sins. The New Testament introduces this Savior as Jesus Christ, the perfect, sinless man who is God, and who would die on a cross to pay the penalty for our sins. Jesus would then rise from the dead three days after His death, an act which would show the world He is God and He has conquered death for those of us who put our faith and trust in Him.

Here is where the problem begins. John 14:6 says:

Jesus said to him, "I am the way, and the truth, and the life; no one comes to the Father but through Me."

Acts 4:12 adds:

> **"Salvation is found in no one else, for there is no other name under heaven given to men by which we must be saved."**

Jesus claims He alone is the way to God; nothing you do could ever add on to what He has done for you. Religions of today will tell you that yes, Jesus did this for you, **but** you have to work your way to heaven. Religions of today will tell you that you can never be assured of your salvation – that hopefully the good things in your life will outweigh the bad things. Religions tell you that you have to be in church so many times a week, you have to "do" what the church tells you, you have to wear certain clothes, and you have to obey the church rules. Religion says, "I have to work and work for the church and hopefully it will be good enough." Jesus says in Matthew 11:28-30 :

> **"Come to Me, all who are weary and heavy-laden, and I will give you rest. Take My yoke upon you and learn from Me, for I am gentle and humble in heart, and you will find rest for your souls. For My yoke is easy and My burden is light."**

Jesus did not come to make your life miserable. He did not come so you would have to work and add on to what He has done. Our pastor once said in a sermon that Jesus died for the church so we wouldn't have to! How true that is. When we start to add on to what Jesus did on the cross, we have crossed the line on what true, biblical Christianity is.

The bottom line is Jesus died to pay the penalty for our sins.When we turn to Him in repentance and faith, we become so grateful for what He has done for us; so if we feed the homeless, we do it out of gratitude to Jesus. If we teach Sunday school, we do it out of gratitude to Jesus. If we help someone who is hurting, we do it out of gratitude to Jesus. Do you see the difference? We are not doing these things to earn our way to heaven. We are not doing these things because a church is telling us we have to. We do these things because it is an outflow of our love for Jesus who died for us so we could have eternal life with Him.

If you feel like you are joined to a "right tree," look at these statements and see if they apply to you. If so, we beg you to search the truth in the Bible to see if it is possible that you are attached to the "wrong tree."

"The church says I have to believe what they tell me regardless of whether it is in the Bible or not"

"The church tells me the traditions of the church supersede what the Bible says."

"The church tells me I need to believe in other writings other than the Bible alone."

"The church says I have to do this certain job because they feel it is my calling or duty."

"The church says in order to go to heaven I have to attend a certain number of times a week."

"The church says I have to wear certain clothing in order to be a part of them."

"The church says I can never be assured I am going to heaven."

"The church tells me in order to go to heaven I must join with them."

"The church tells me if I'm not a good person, I won't go to heaven."

"The church tells me if I have committed a certain sin that I

cannot go to heaven."

"*The church tells me if I do not get baptized or confirmed in their church I won't go to heaven.*"

The "right tree" is the tree that is Jesus alone. You go to church so you can learn what the Bible teaches. You work at the church because God has gifted you with singing, working with children teaching, or serving others. You do these things because you love Jesus and you want to serve Him. He has given you these abilities to serve in His church. The minute someone begins telling you what you have to "do" in order to belong to God, then you need to take a second look at the church you are attending.

God is serious about His Word being the final authority in your life. Anything added to His Word would assure you that you are attached to the "wrong tree." This is serious to us. I (Lisa) was talking to a woman one day and we were discussing what the Bible said versus what her religion taught her. I asked her if she had ever read the Bible and she responded by saying, "I leave that up to my priest to tell me what to believe." This is the problem; we want our church leaders to tell us what the truth is without ever checking it out ourselves.

When we were at the lake this summer, we handed our first book "Got Heaven" to a young man who was fueling the boat. A few days later he came up to us and started talking. He told us he was getting ready to go on a mission trip, but seemed very confused on what he truly believed. We came back a few days later with some information on *his religion* showing him the differences between what his religion taught and what the *Bible* truly said. In the course of the conversation, we explained to him that if his religion was right, we would probably end up in an okay place – maybe not the highest place – but an okay place, but if the Bible was right, then he would spend eternity in hell separated from God. He was a nice person who wanted to serve God. He was so sincere and wanted to devote his life to Him. He believed his church and their doctrine and books that had been added to the Bible over the Bible. He was getting ready to go away and give his life to a church, but he wasn't grounded in the Bible well enough to refute what he was being taught.

We challenge you to open the Bible for yourselves and read it. This is not a **church** problem, this is a **salvation** problem. If you place your faith and trust in a church that teaches anything other than what the Bible teaches, you are attached to the "wrong tree". You may be the nicest person, go to church more than anyone you know, help out every weekend at the shelters, give away most of your money, never use bad language, never watch television or go to the movies, but you could be headed for eternal separation from God because you have placed your faith in the "wrong tree."

Salvation is a gift from God, not something we work for ourselves. Has anyone ever given you a gift, and in return, you paid them back for it? If you are trying to be good enough or work for the church hard enough, then, in essence, you are trying to pay God back for giving you a gift. That is not what salvation is about. Ephesians 2:8-9 says:

"For it is by grace you have been saved, through faith— and this not from yourselves, it is the gift of God— not by works, so that no one can boast."

We are to do nice things for people and love others because it proves we have faith in Christ. We don't work for God in order to work our way to heaven. James 2:18-20 says:

14

"But someone may well say, 'You have faith and I have works; show me your faith without the works, and I will show you my faith by my works'. You believe that God is one. You do well; the demons also believe, and shudder. But are you willing to recognize, you foolish fellow, that faith without works is useless?"

Ephesians 2:10 also makes this point:

"For we are God's workmanship, created in Christ Jesus to do good works, which God prepared in advance for us to do."

When we become Christians, we don't just sit around and do nothing. God has given us gifts and jobs to do. We now have a new boss and it is our job to obey what He tells us to do. The difference is that we are attached to Jesus, we read His Word (which tells us how to live), and our lives begin to change with true fruit since we are attached to the true tree. Many people can produce what looks like fruit; they can be nice and do good things, but if they are doing it to work their way to heaven or because a church tells them to, they are producing false fruit. In Arizona, we have orange trees that produce fake oranges. They look like the real thing, but they taste awful - they have no value as fruit. The same holds true for us if we are attached to the wrong tree. We may look good, but we are not real because we are not attached to Jesus, the One who produces the real fruit in our lives.

Please check out your belief system. Look at what John 15:1-8 says:

"I am the true vine, and my Father is the gardener. He cuts off every branch in me that bears no fruit, while every branch that does bear fruit he prunes so that it will

be even more fruitful. You are already clean because of the word I have spoken to you. Remain in me, and I will remain in you. No branch can bear fruit by itself; it must remain in the vine. Neither can you bear fruit unless you remain in me. I am the vine; you are the branches. If a man remains in me and I in him, he will bear much fruit; apart from me you can do nothing. If anyone does not remain in me, he is like a branch that is thrown away and withers; such branches are picked up, thrown into the fire and burned. If you remain in me and my words remain in you, ask whatever you wish, and it will be given you. This is to my Father's glory, that you bear much fruit, showing yourselves to be my disciples."

Another concern we have for people who produce pretend and plastic fruit is they assume it is real. We know many people who do nice things for others: they give money to charity, they feed the homeless. We were just watching a program on TV the other night and one girl gave away her three million dollar inheritance to charity! These people have one problem – they are attached to the wrong tree - maybe it is a "religious tree," maybe it is a "philanthropy tree," maybe they are attached to a "good works tree" or a "tradition tree". Maybe they are just nice people and feel they will get to heaven because of the nice things they do. The Bible is clear – if we are not attached to the right tree, it doesn't matter what we do in our lives. It is meaningless. It is worthless. The only tree that means anything is the "Jesus" tree, and the only fruit worth producing is what we do because of our faith in Him.

There is salvation in NO OTHER than Jesus Christ and Jesus Christ alone.

CHAPTER 2

FACTS ABOUT FRUIT TREES

As we studied fruit trees for this book, we came upon some interesting facts that could be applied to our lives as Christians. Here are a few:

1. **_A fruit tree will bear fruit for 20-60 years._** Fruit doesn't stop! This is a hard concept for many people to understand. Many people believe as long as they just "believe in Jesus" that their responsibility to grow stops. They don't understand that as a Christian you will bear fruit and it will continue. Just like a fruit tree bears fruit for many years, so we as Christians are to do the same. The Bible makes it clear that a person will be known as a Christian by what their life is producing. For instance, Matthew 7:16 says: **"You will know them by their fruits."**

We are in a small group which is filled with all different age groups. By far the group that touches our hearts the most is the older generation. They get it. They understand what it means to walk with the Lord, to produce fruit. They are there to answer the tough questions for us. They are there to guide us through the tough times. They have the fruit of love and patience and gentleness and our lives are measurably richer for knowing them and seeing the fruit that is produced by their close attachment to Christ.

Clearly, we are **known** to be believers if we bear fruit, so what about those that say they are Christians and yet have no signs of fruit in their life? We talk to people who tell us their so-called "Christian" spouse is divorcing them for no apparent biblical reason. We read an article in a magazine yesterday of a guy who is in a popular band and just informed everyone he was gay. When asked if he would still go to church, he responded he would because he was still a Christian. So, here is the question: if someone is living in a continual, unrepentant lifestyle that goes directly against what God calls fruit – disobedience to His word, unloving and greedy, unkind words being spoken, lies and slander abounding, unrighteous act, does the Bible say this person is truly a Christian? To become a Christian means you humbly come before a holy God in REPENTANCE and FAITH, an act that requires turning from the old lifestyles we just wrote about.

> **James 2:18-20 says, But someone may well say, "You have faith and I have works; show me your faith without the works, and I will show you my faith by my works." You believe that God is one. You do well; the demons also believe, and shudder. But are you willing to recognize, you foolish fellow, that faith without works is useless?**

This verse makes it abundantly clear: you will be known as a Christian by your actions or your fruit. A Christian turns his life over to Christ, reads His commands, OBEYS His commands, and produces fruit. Anything less would be a false version of Christianity.

Matthew 7:13-14 says, "Enter by the narrow gate; for wide is the gate and broad is the way that leads to destruction, and there are many who go in by it. Because narrow is the gate and difficult is the way which leads to life, and there are few who find it."

Remember what Matthew 7 says – the road is NARROW. The narrow road which produces fruit would consist of obedience to God's Word. Jesus goes on to say in **Matthew 7:17-20, "Even so, every good tree bears good fruit, but a bad tree bears bad fruit. A good tree cannot bear bad fruit, nor can a bad tree bear good fruit. Every tree that does not bear good fruit is cut down and thrown into the fire. Therefore by their fruits you will know them."**

What about us? A fruit tree naturally bears fruit, so as believers in Christ and being attached to Him, what are our lives producing?

2. *Growth patterns are determined by pruning and training.*
Fruit grows as the tree is trained and pruned. In our lives, when God shows us a particular sin from His Word, are we trained by it? Do we continue in the same lifestyle, or do we repent and turn away from it? Our growth in our relationship with Christ will come directly from what we learn in His Word and how obedient we are to what He asks of us.

1 Corinthians 6:9-10 tells us,
> **"Do you not know that the unrighteous will not inherit the kingdom of God? Do not be deceived.**
> **Neither fornicators, nor idolaters, nor adulterers,**
> **nor homosexuals, nor sodomites, nor thieves, nor**
> **covetous, nor drunkards, nor revilers, nor extortioners**

will inherit the kingdom of God."

When we are taught that these things are displeasing to the Lord, then through the power of the Holy Spirit, we are to stop. If we live in a *continual* pattern of these actions without any conviction to change, then we need to check ourselves to see if we are in the faith. On the other hand, if we read these things and use His Words to train ourselves, we will know how He calls us to act as His children. Just as our children go to school to be trained in math and english, so God uses the Bible to train us as to what it means to be His.

3. *If the tree is exposed, you will need to have protections from strong winds.* If you are a new believer, you will need protection from the world, protection from sinful influences, protection from the things Satan will throw your way. The way you receive this protection is through your church and through other believers. You need the body of Christ to come around you and help you grow and learn God's Word. You need true believers who will be there when times get tough. These needs are usually met by joining a small group within your church or a small Bible study where you can share your life with others. This will help protect you from the strong winds that will come along to try and derail your faith.

Hebrews 10:24-25 says, **"and let us consider how to stimulate one another to love and good deeds, not forsaking our own assembling together, as is the habit of some, but encouraging one another; and all the more as you see the day drawing near."**

Acts 14:21-22 tells us, **"And when they had preached the gospel to that city and made many disciples, they returned to Lystra, Iconium, and Antioch, strengthening the souls**

of the disciples, exhorting them to continue in the faith, and saying, "We must through many tribulations enter the kingdom of God."

The Bible teaches us that as a Christian we WILL have trials and tribulation. If you became a Christian because someone told you that you would live a problem-free existence, you were not told the truth. The Bible is clear that believers will have problems. When we take a stand for the Bible as our final authority, that will surely cause problems. When we take a stand on divorce, adultery, homosexuality, and holy living, the world will have problems with us. Suddenly, we are being called "judgmental," or "hypocritical," for taking the stand we do. If you live with someone who is not a believer, your world has just gotten a lot more difficult. But God calls us to stand strong, to persevere, and to stand for the truth. That is hard to do, and yet He promises in **2 Corinthians 12:8-10, Concerning this thing I pleaded with the Lord three times that it might depart from me. And He said to me, "My grace is sufficient for you, for My strength is made perfect in weakness." Therefore most gladly I will rather boast in my infirmities, that the power of Christ may rest upon me. Therefore I take pleasure in infirmities, in reproaches, in needs, in persecutions, in distresses, for Christ's sake. For when I am weak, then I am strong.**

4. *__Make a plan.__* Just as a gardener has to have a plan to help a tree grow, we as Christians need a plan on how to grow, also. This plan would always include time reading your Bible each day, being in a church that teaches God's Word, praying, and finding friends who love God and His Word. As believers, we need a plan on how to grow as Christians. **Acts 2:42** makes it clear that when 3,000 people became Christians, they did this: **"They were continually**

devoting themselves to the apostles' teaching and to fellowship, to the breaking of bread and to prayer."

After becoming Christians, they studied God's Word, had fellowship with other believers, took communion, and spent their time in prayer. That is what a Christian life looks like. Somewhere along the line, we were fed a false notion that we don't need to go to church or read our Bibles. Somewhere along the line, someone told us that church was not important – besides, we only have the weekend to do chores or go to the lake. Somewhere along the line, the plan God had for us to grow in our faith got distorted and watered down. We have to come back to what the apostles said to us about how important these things are. Psalm 119:11 says, **"Your Word I have hidden in my heart, that I might not sin against You."**

The Bible is our lifeline to teach us what God wants for us. We need to be reading it every day of our lives for the rest of our lives. We hear of people all the time who say they "read the Bible through a long time ago" and they haven't picked it up in years. God says in Hebrews 4:12, **"For the word of God is living and powerful, and sharper than any two-edged sword, piercing even to the division of soul and spirit, and of joints and marrow, and is a discerner of the thoughts and intents of the heart."**

The Bible is alive and as we read it in different stages of our life, it teaches us different things each day. Have a plan, read your Bible, and pray each day for the issues in your life and for your friends and family. Find a good Bible-teaching church and make a commitment to go each week. Make a plan just like the gardener who has to make a plan to plant a tree. Make a plan to grow spiritually.

When we were at the beach this summer, I (Lisa) decided to go walking on the beach early in the morning. I saw a woman who was running effortlessly and for a long distance, and I wanted to stop her and ask her why she did this. Why would a person take the time out of their busy schedule, run up and down the beach, get all hot and sweaty, and then drive all the way home? Once they get home, they have to take a shower and get ready for the day. Why would anyone do this? We assume it is because of the benefits. She looked great, had energy, and was in great shape. The same goes for us as we make a plan to grow closer to God. As we do things like read and pray, the benefits of knowing Him and growing closer to Him are worth far more than the time and effort it takes us.

5. _Water._ A tree has to have water to grow. The Bible says Jesus is our "living water." As Christians we know Jesus is the only way to God and that a relationship with Him is the key to being a true believer, but for the idea of growth, we will use the Bible as our water. We cannot grow in our faith if we are not reading each day to see what God calls us to do. If we are not being watered each day, just like a tree, our faith will end up dying. Just like the parable of the seeds, some seeds never make it because they are never watered or nurtured or they are thrown in places that they can't thrive. To grow in our faith we have to be reading our Bibles each day.

One of our children left for college a few years back, and before he left he thought he might go into the ministry. But as he got involved in college life and fraternity life, the things of God became less and less important to him. After he graduated, I (Rob) went to him and challenged him to read the New Testament in a year. It literally changed his life. Somehow in the incredible wisdom of God, He uses His Word and the Holy Spirit to change our lives. That is why throughout this book we will constantly bring the idea of bearing fruit back to reading your Bibles. Apart from His Word, true fruit cannot be produced.

Psalm 1 says, **"How blessed is the man who does not walk in the counsel of the wicked, nor stand in the path of sinners, nor sit in the seat of scoffers! But his delight is in the law of the Lord, and in His law he meditates day and night. He will be like a tree firmly planted by streams of water, which yields its fruit in its season and its leaf does not wither; and in whatever he does, he prospers. The wicked are not so, but they are like chaff which the wind drives away. Therefore the wicked will not stand in the judgment, nor sinners in the assembly of the right-eous. For the Lord knows the way of the righteous, but the way of the wicked will perish."**

6. Check your soil. Just as a tree has to be planted in good soil, so do Christians need to be planted in a good church. Soil is such an important part of growth – the condition of it directly determines if the tree will grow. In the same way, the church you become involved with matters greatly. It can determine whether you will grow in your faith or not. If you attend a church that spends most of the time only talking about God's love, wanting to make sure you are always happy, and never confronts your sin, then you are in a "soft soil" church and you will never grow the proper way. If you go to a church that gives you lists of rules and regulations that the church believes but can't be backed up by Scripture, then you would be going to a "hard soil" church and you will end up trying to be a Christian by doing what the church tells you to do instead of serving out of a love for Jesus through the power of the Holy Spirit.

The "good soil" church is one that understands and teaches God is holy and righteous. It is a church that shows God's hatred of sin and how He wants us to repent and turn from the things that offend Him. It is a church that understands God's grace and forgivness. It is a church that shows us God loves us so much that he sent Jesus to die on a cross to pay the penalty for our sins, but that because of what He did for us, our lives should be filled with humility and gratitude for that love and sacrifice. It is a church that stands by what the Bible says regardless of what the culture says. It is a church that understands we are there to worship a holy God and teaches us that we are here to serve God. It is a place that is all about **"God"** and not about **"me."**

When we come to a place where we understand what it truly means to be a Christian, then church is not a place we go for our own personal fulfillment. We are there to worship Jesus who saved us. We are there to learn about this awesome God. We are there to serve. Many people believe church is there to fulfill their needs, but in reality, we are there to serve others. Children's ministry? Nursery? Parking attendant? Serving donuts? Singing in the choir? Whatever God has gifted you with is what you need to be doing as a service to your church.

> **Ephesians 4:11-13** makes this clear: **"And He gave some as apostles, and some as prophets, and some as evangelists, and some as pastors and teachers, for the equipping of the saints for the work of service, to the building up of the body of Christ; until we all attain to the unity of the faith, and of the knowledge of the Son of God, to a mature man, to the measure of the stature which belongs to the fullness of Christ."**

CHAPTER 3

FACTS ABOUT TREE PRUNING

When a gardener prunes a tree, he is trying to achieve certain goals to help the tree grow up into a healthy tree. Here are a few goals of a gardener.

1. Shaping a young tree. When we become Christians, God begins working in our hearts to shape us into people who will look like Jesus. Romans 8:29 says,

> **"For those whom He foreknew, He also predestined to become conformed to the image of His Son, so that He would be the firstborn among many brethren;"**

He also wants us to look like "lights" to a very dark world.

Matthew 5:14-16 says, "You are the light of the world. A city that is set on a hill cannot be hidden. Nor do they light a lamp and put it under a basket, but on a lampstand, and it gives light to all who are in the house. Let your light so shine before men, that they may see your good works and glorify your Father in heaven."

When we read His Word, He will use what it says to shape us and change us. He will reveal sin to us so we can repent and turn away from it. An example would be that you were raised believing it was okay to have sex before you were married, but as you read the Bible, you begin to understand God never intended sex outside a marriage relationship. The result is that He shapes you as you understand His Word and changes you from the ideas you were raised with to the truth He calls you to live by. Maybe you lived with a family who spent most of their time talking about people behind their backs, but now as you read the Bible, you learn that God does not want us to gossip. Again, we are shaped as we learn what God wants from us, and out of our love for Him, we obey what He says through the power of the Holy Spirit living in us.

*2. **Producing new growth where desired.*** As we grow in our walk with the Lord, He begins to produce new thought patterns and attitudes in our lives. He produces love and forgiveness where there once was hate and anger. He produces a desire for holy living where there once was a desire to do only "what I wanted." He produces an obedient lifestyle that replaces a disobedient one. As we stay attached to Jesus and as we read His Word, God will then produce the things in our lives He desires.

*3. **Correct or repair damage.*** When a gardener needs to correct a tree, he prunes it and cuts back what shouldn't be there. In the same way, God corrects us when we disobey Him. The Bible says in **Hebrews 12:7-8, "It is for discipline that you endure; God deals with you as with sons; for what son is there whom his father does not discipline? But if you are without discipline, of which all have become partakers, then you are illegitimate children and not sons."**

If you can live in a continual, unrepentant, life of sin without ever being disciplined, you might want to check and see if your faith is genuine. There has to be growth and there has to be correction. Just like a father who wants his son to grow up and be a responsible child, so God our Father wants us to be His responsible children. His discipline produces change in us to help further our growth to look more like Jesus.

4. *Helps control and prevent insects and diseases*. Just like the gardener who does not want his tree infected with diseases, God does not want His children infected with sin.

James 1:14-15 tells us, **"But each one is tempted when he is carried away and enticed by his own lust. Then when lust has conceived, it gives birth to sin; and when sin is accomplished, it brings forth death."**

Diseases can end in death. James makes the point that when we are tempted to do something against what God would call us to do, we have a choice. If we choose to disobey God and fall to the temptation, then that act gives birth to sin which in the long run brings forth death. As we read God's Word, we are taught temptation is not sin – we will always have temptation in our lives, but when we succumb to the temptation, it becomes sin and that is the very thing God is trying to keep us from. He knows how diseases hurt people and He always has our best interests in mind. Just as the gardener tries to prevent his tree from being affected by insects and diseases, so God does the same for us by warning us in the Bible how sin affects our life and the lives of others around us.

Have you ever known someone who committed adultery? Have you seen the destruction and devastation left behind from it? Have you seen the loss of their marriage, the loss of respect from their children? Have you seen distrust and unforgiveness? These are consequences of sin that God wants to protect us from, and if we obey Him and do what He says, these kinds of consequences won't affect our lives. All sin produces pain, but if we live a life of obedience to what God asks of us, our lives will be free of this dysfunction.

5. *Rejuvenate or reshape an older plant.* Maybe you are older and have felt like you have been a Christian for a long time, but you are not growing. Maybe you have been complacent about your faith, and God is trying to get your attention. Maybe you are having trials in your life and you don't understand what is going on. What is going on? God is trying to rejuvenate you and reshape your life! Have you lost the desire to worship in church? Are you still reading your Bible each day? Have your hobbies become more important than the things of God? Do you ache for the salvation of your unsaved friends or family? God wants us to grow in Him until the day we die. He wants us to understand what it means to be a Christian and how that changes our lives. He wants us to understand that our faith has to be "lasting." It doesn't just stop or slow down when we get older.

As we get older, we should be MORE knowledgeable about God's Word, we should care MORE for the salvation of our unsaved friends and family members, and we should care MORE for the body of Christ. As we get older our faith should be stronger not weaker. We should love Jesus more than we did when we first came to know Him. If none of this is happening in your life, we beg you to check your life spiritually. If you are older and are not growing, please consider what **2 Corinthians 13:5** says: **"Test yourselves to see if you are in the faith; examine yourselves! Or do you not recognize this about yourselves, that Jesus Christ is in you— unless indeed you fail the test?"**

Revelation 2:4-5 says, **"But I have this against you, that you have left your first love. 'Therefore remember from where you have fallen, and repent and do the deeds you did at first; or else I am coming to you and will remove your lampstand out of its place—unless you repent."**

A true believer is in a growth pattern, producing more and more fruit as he grows. If there is no fruit being produced in your life, you need to make sure you understand what it means to be a TRUE believer in Jesus. It changes everything in your life. If you feel you have left your first love, the love you once had for Jesus, He asks you to repent. Turn back to Him. He is waiting for you.

*6. **Increase the production, size and quality of fruit.*** As a tree is being pruned, it enables the fruit to increase in its size and quality. Awhile back, I (Rob) was in a meeting and I heard one of the shop guys ask his boss what was more important to the company - quantity or quality. His boss said he wanted both. That is what God wants from us. As He shows us more and more what He wants from us and as we obey more and more the **quantity** of our love, joy, peace, and patience will grow. As we grow in our relationship with Christ the **quality** of our love, joy, peace, and patience will grow, also.

If He wants us to learn to love people more, that might mean God will put a very unlovable person in our lives to teach us the true meaning of love. If He wants us to be more joyful, He might put trials in our lives so we can learn how to be joyful in tough situations. If He wants us to learn how to have peace in all situations, He might allow us to go through a time where we lose a job or lose our health. God uses all of these trials in our lives to help us grow in our relationship with Him and produce more and more fruit along the way.

CHAPTER 4

CAN I PRODUCE FRUIT ON MY OWN?

What does fruit in a person look like? Have you ever wondered how fruit is produced? Can I do this on my own, or does something have to happen in order for this to be produced in my life? As we were working through what it means to have what the Bible calls "fruit," we came up with a thought. Fruit would be as follows:

Any righteous living that comes from abiding in Christ.

How does this work? When people come to the realization that they are sinners separated from a holy God, turn to Him in repentance and faith, and relinquish their lives to Christ, they become as John 3:3 says "born again." Here are some exciting things that happen when a person becomes a Christian.

Ephesians 1:13-14 says,

"In Him, you also, after listening to the message of truth, the gospel of your salvation—having also believed, you were sealed in Him with the Holy Spirit of promise, who

is given as a pledge of our inheritance, with a view to the redemption of God's own possession, to the praise of His glory."

YOU ARE GUANATEED THE HOLY SPIRIT
WILL LIVE IN YOU!

Ephesians 2:8-9 says,

"For by grace you have been saved through faith, and that not of yourselves; it is the gift of God, not of works, lest anyone should boast."

YOU ARE SAVED BECAUSE GOD BESTOWED
THIS GIFT OF SALVATION TO YOU!

Ephesians 2:1-5 says,

"And you were dead in your trespasses and sins, in which you formerly walked according to the course of this world, according to the prince of the power of the air, of the spirit that is now working in the sons of disobedience. Among them we too all formerly lived in the lusts of our flesh, indulging the desires of the flesh and of the mind, and were by nature children of wrath, even as the rest. But God, being rich in mercy, because of His great love with which He loved us, even when we were dead in our transgressions, made us alive together with Christ (by grace you have been saved)."

WE WERE DEAD IN SIN AND CHRIST MADE
US ALIVE IN HIM!

Ephesians 2:13 says,

"But now in Christ Jesus you who formerly were far off

have been brought near by the blood of Christ."

THE BLOOD OF CHRIST HAS BROUGHT
US NEAR TO HIM!

So many things happened when we became Christians! God saved us, moved us from the darkness to the light, and gave us His Holy Spirit to live within us. The power of the Holy Spirit is what is going to produce fruit in our lives. We cannot do this on our own; understand that it will be the Holy Spirit who produces in us what God expects from us. As a new Christian, it can be so defeating trying to live a life that is pleasing to God. Ephesians 4:1 tells us:

"Therefore I, the prisoner of the Lord, implore you to walk in a manner worthy of the calling with which you have been called,"

How can I walk worthy of this calling? How can I begin to produce the things in my life that God asks of me? Here is the answer… RELAX! We have grapefruit trees at our house, and never once have we gone out to watch the grapefruits work to grow! We have never seen these grapefruit strain and groan to become more of a grapefruit. You know what the grapefruit does? It stays attached to the branches, which is attached to the tree which is being fed and watered. Therein lays the answer to the problem of spiritual growth and of producing fruit: abide. Stay attached to the tree. Be in church, read your Bible daily, be fed by His Word, let the Holy Spirit work in your life the things that are pleasing to Him and work out of your life the things that displease Him. You do your part to stay attached to the right tree and you will be amazed at how your life will start to change. Old attitudes of hatred and bitterness will be changed to love and forgiveness. Old habits of worry and anxiety will be changed to peace and joy.

Growth takes time. We do not walk out one day and suddenly see a grapefruit that grew overnight. It takes time to become a fully grown grapefruit just like it takes years and years to become a fully grown Christian. In reality, it takes a lifetime. We will never fully arrive where God wants us to be until we are with Him in heaven. That is part of living on this earth, living in these earthly, bodies always fighting the things of the flesh against the things of the Spirit but know one thing: Philippians 1:6 says:

"For I am confident of this very thing, that He who began a good work in you will perfect it until the day of Christ Jesus."

God has begun this work in you and it is He that will finish it. The Holy Spirit will produce this fruit in us as we spend time immersed in His Word. Hebrews 4:12 says:

"For the word of God is living and active and sharper than any two-edged sword, and piercing as far as the division of soul and spirit, of both joints and marrow, and able to judge the thoughts and intentions of the heart."

God's Word pierces our soul; it discerns the thoughts and intents of our heart. It shows us who we really are, it shows us our motives. The Bible is how God changes us. As we read it, the Holy Spirit convicts us of the things that do not please God and enables us to change. Have you ever seen this at work? Have you ever had someone in your life who wanted nothing to do with God and then experienced a whole life change after becoming a Christian? It is an amazing testimony of how the Spirit of God through the Word of God changes lives.

2 Timothy 3:16 also sheds more light on what the Bible does in our life.

"All Scripture is inspired by God and profitable for teaching, for reproof, for correction, for training in righteousness,..."

As we break this verse apart, we see that the Bible was given to us for "doctrine," that is, it teaches us if what we believe in is true. So many religions have their own doctrines and traditions which do not align with what the Bible teaches. That is why the Bible has to be our final authority. We have to read it to know what God wants us to believe in, not what a pastor, radio station, or church tells us to believe in.

"Reproof" is the second thing the Bible is useful for in growing a Christian. This means the Bible will show us what behavior is wrong and what patterns of thinking are against what He is calling for in us. If you were raised thinking that living together before marriage was a good thing, but as you read God's Word He shows you that your thinking was not based on a biblical context, that is reproof.

"Correction" is the third part of this verse and it means the Bible will teach us how to get back to where God wants us to be. God uses His Word to correct our wrong thinking and bad attitudes.

The last part of this verse tells us the Bible is used for "instruction in righteousness," which means it shows us how to live a godly life. It instructs us on how we do things like produce fruit, be kind to others, or love God with all our hearts. The Holy Spirit uses the Word of God as a change agent. For example, if you had never read your Bible and you read Galatians 5:19-21, you might be convicted if you were living any of these lifestyles:

"Now the deeds of the flesh are evident, which are: immorality, impurity, sensuality, idolatry, sorcery, enmities, strife, jealousy, outbursts of anger, disputes, dissensions, factions, envying, drunkenness, carousing, and things like these, of which I forewarn you, just as I have fore-warned you, that those who practice such things will not inherit the kingdom of God."

You might be shocked to see these lifestyles or practices are forbidden as a Christian. Suddenly, you realize you can't have an adulterous affair, you can't have sex before marriage, you can't be jealous, and you can't be going out getting drunk on the weekends. He doesn't tell you this because He wants to spoil all your fun, but because He wants to protect you. As the Holy Spirit shows you these things, a choice needs to be made on your part: either continue in sin or repent and obey. The Bible says if you are a Christian, one of the things that will happen to you is you now have the ability to say "no" to the things that displease God. Out of obedience to God, you walk away from that affair, you stop sleeping with the person you aren't married to. Now you can say "no." These are tough issues. The Bible says these things about obedience:

John 15:14:
"You are My friends if you do what I command you."

John 14:15:
"If you love Me, you will keep My commandments."

Matthew 7:21-23:
"Not everyone who says to Me, 'Lord, Lord,' will enter

the kingdom of heaven, but he who does the will of My Father who is in heaven will enter. "Many will say to Me on that day, 'Lord, Lord, did we not prophesy in Your name, and in Your name cast out demons, and in Your name perform many miracles?' "And then I will declare to them, 'I never knew you; depart from Me, you who practice lawlessness.'"

These verses explain that if we love Jesus, we will want to obey Him. Obedience might mean walking away from a relationship that is wrong or a lifestyle that is not what God asks of you. That is obedience. If you are struggling with obeying His Word, you need to be honest with God. He knows your heart, He knows if you truly want to change. He promises this in 1 Corinthians 10:12-13:

"Therefore let him who thinks he stands take heed that he does not fall. No temptation has overtaken you but such as is common to man; and God is faithful, who will not allow you to be tempted beyond what you are able, but with the temptation will provide the way of escape also, so that you will be able to endure it."

God promises that since you are a Christian, you will be able to walk away from things that displease Him. He will give you the power and the ability to turn your back and repent from what He calls wrong. As you fill your mind with God's Word and prayerfully tell Him how hard this is for you, He promises to make a way of escape for you. We know people who used to live a lifestyle disobedient to God's Word, and yet God has changed their hearts and minds so drastically that to do the things they used to would be appalling to them now! The parties they used to love are depressing and lonely. The gossip at the girl's night out isn't much fun anymore. The relationship based on sex is not exciting anymore.

Instead, they want to talk about the things of God; they want to share Him with others. The things they used to want and like to do don't even appeal to them anymore! Why? Romans 12:2 has the answer:

"And do not be conformed to this world, but be transformed by the renewing of your mind, so that you may prove what the will of God is, that which is good and acceptable and perfect."

God will renew your mind. He will change the way you think so that what you think and how you act is now acceptable to God. God calls us to be different, and that can only happen as we *abide, read and pray.* Before we look at what fruit in your life should look like, let's look at what fruit is not. This will give us a chance to examine our lives to see if anything unhealthy is being produced in our lives so we can ask God to change us from the inside out.

CHAPTER 5

WHAT FRUIT IS NOT!

As we look at Galatians 5:19-21, we will notice that these deeds are produced by the flesh and God says these actions are not conducive of a Christian. This is what the Bible says is produced by the flesh in Galatians 5:19-21:

> **"Now the deeds of the flesh are evident, which are: immorality, impurity, sensuality, idolatry, sorcery, enmities, strife, jealousy, outbursts of anger, disputes, dissensions, factions, envying, drunkenness, carousing, and things like these, of which I forewarn you, just as I have fore-warned you, that those who practice such things will not inherit the kingdom of God."**

The second list in Galatians 5:22-23 is what the Spirit produces in our lives:

> **"But the fruit of the Spirit is love, joy, peace, patience, kindness, goodness, faithfulness, gentleness and self-control; against such things there is no law."**

The first list contains activities and actions that a child of God neither exhibits nor desires. This verse says those who practice these things will not inherit the Kingdom of God. If you are living in any of these lifestyles, you need to check yourself to see if you really are in the faith. The problem is this, do all of us at one time or another act jealous, act selfish, and have outbursts of anger? Do we envy others or have impure thoughts? Do we have people or hobbies in our lives that are considered an idol? Does that mean we aren't Christians? The answer here is twofold.

First, the New King James Version of verse 21 says those who "practice such things will not inherit the kingdom of God." This means a continuous action – something that can go on continually in your life without any thought of turning from these sins. If you are a Christian and you have these thoughts or actions, you should be convicted about these behaviors. Upon realizing these actions do not align with how God calls you to act, you confess and repent. What this verse is saying is that a Christian cannot live with these continued actions without a repentant heart. If you can live like this list without feeling any guilt or shame, you need to examine your life.

Second, if you are a new Christian and you live in an adulterous lifestyle or you spend your weekends going to parties and getting drunk, please understand you have just begun this "new life." There is a battle going on inside of you; the flesh and its actions are fighting against this new life God wants you to live. If you read your Bible and pray and want God to change you, don't be discouraged! These changes don't usually happen overnight. God will take each area in your life that is displeasing to Him and work that out. If you have recently given your life to Christ and went out last weekend and got drunk, that does not necessarily mean you are not a Christian. How you would determine that would be by asking yourself, "Did I feel bad for what I did?" "Did I hurt those around me and feel the need to apologize?" "Did I realize as a Christian God does not want me to live that lifestyle?" If these questions bother you, that would be the Holy Spirit working in your life, showing you your actions are not advancing your new life in Christ.

Find someone in your church that can come along side of you and help you and pray for you when the temptation seems hard to bear. Being a Christian is not something you can do on your own. Remember what Paul said in **Romans 7:15 -25,**

"For what I am doing, I do not understand; for I am not practicing what I would like to do, but I am doing the very thing I hate. But if I do the very thing I do not want to do, I agree with the Law, confessing that the Law is good. So now, no longer am I the one doing it, but sin which dwells in me. For I know that nothing good dwells in me, that is, in my flesh; for the willing is present in me, but the doing of the good is not. For the good that I want, I do not do, but I practice the very evil that I do not want. But if I am doing the very thing I do not want, I am no longer the one doing it, but sin which dwells in me. I find then the principle that evil is present in me, the one who wants to do good. For I joyfully concur with the law of God in the inner man, but I see a different law in the members of my body, waging war against the law of my mind and making me a prisoner of the law of sin which is in my members. Wretched man that I am! Who will set me free from the body of this death? Thanks be to God through Jesus Christ our Lord! So then, on the one hand I myself with my mind am serving the law of God, but on the other, with my flesh the law of sin."

The second list from Galatians 5:22-23 is what God will start replacing the things in the first list with from Galatians 5:19-21. For instance, if you have an affair, the Holy Spirit will convict you of this sin, you will have the ability to walk away from this destructive pattern and He will give you self control, faithfulness, and kindness. If you get angry at your spouse or your children, you will have the ability to apologize to them, and God will begin to replace this action with self control, love, patience, and kindness. Once you begin to see in list one what you are doing that is displeasing to God, then you need to pray and ask God to take away these things that He does not want in your life. You need to be in constant prayer. Ask for God to make you aware if your actions are not how He would call you to now live. You will be amazed at how He will change you from the inside out.

Ezekiel 36:26 -27 "Moreover, I will give you a new heart and put a new spirit within you; and I will remove the heart of stone from your flesh and give you a heart of flesh. I will put My Spirit within you and cause you to walk in My statutes, and you will be careful to observe My ordinances."

Remember this: only as you are abiding in Him can HE do this in your life. Admit you cannot change on your own. When you recognize a sin pattern in your life, go before the Lord and ask Him to help you change. Keep an attitude of prayer, and read your Bible daily. Eventually, you will be saddened by your own behavior. This is evidence that God is slowly working the sinful things out of your life and replacing them with what He wants you to be.

A SECOND LIST!

We will go through this list one action at a time to get a better idea of what fruit is "not." 2 Timothy 3:1 -5 says the following:

"But mark this: There will be terrible times in the last days. People will be lovers of themselves, lovers of money, boastful, proud, abusive, disobedient to their parents, ungrateful, unholy, without love, unforgiving, slanderous, without self-control, brutal, not lovers of the good, treacherous, rash, conceited, lovers of pleasure rather than lovers of God— having a form of godliness but denying its power. Have nothing to do with them." (NIV)

Before we begin this second list, please note one thing in verse five. The people who have these traits in their lives have a "form of godliness, but deny its power." What an amazing verse – these are people who are in the churches! The fact they can go to church, talk about God, and yet produce these things in their lives is almost unbelievable.

Recently our son was in a store trying to share the gospel with someone he had met. After talking with the man, he saw a car pull up with a sticker on the back window advertising a church in our area. Our son thought this would be great, hoping the second man would come in and help him talk to the first man about Christ. Instead, this man walked through the door using the foulest language. This gave new meaning to having a "form of godliness (a sticker on your back window) and yet "denying it's power" (the power of the Holy Spirit to be a good witness to unbelievers.)

Matthew 13:24 -30 shows us that true and false Christians grow in the churches together. They look alike. If you get nothing else from this book, get this: our churches today are filled with true and false believers.

"Jesus presented another parable to them, saying, "The kingdom of heaven may be compared to a man who sowed good seed in his field. But while his men were sleeping, his enemy came and sowed tares among the wheat, and went away. But when the wheat sprouted and bore grain, then the tares became evident also."The slaves of the landowner came and said to him, 'Sir, did you not sow good seed in your field? How then does it have tares?' And he said to them, 'An enemy has done this!'The slaves said to him, 'Do you want us, then, to go and gather them up?' But he said, 'No; for while you are gathering up the tares, you may uproot the wheat with them. Allow both to grow together until the harvest; and in the time of the harvest I will say to the reapers, first gather up the tares and bind them in bundles to burn them up; but gather the wheat into my barn."

Here are a few verses to show you there are many people in the churches today who claim to know Christ. They do not. There are many counterfeit Christians in this world, and Satan has placed them in the churches. An ideal way to turn people away from Christ is to have unbelievers in the churches who live how they want, sin when they want, and live unholy lives. When people see these so-called Christians go to church, it gives them a great excuse not to go themselves. We hear it all the time. "Why would I want to join the church when there are so many hypocrites?" "Why would I want to go to church when I see your bumper sticker on your car and yet you drink, swear, and sleep around with your neighbor?" 2 Corinthians 11:26 says:

> **"I have been on frequent journeys, in dangers from
> rivers, dangers from robbers, dangers from my country
> men, dangers from the Gentiles, dangers in the city,
> dangers in the wilderness, dangers on the sea, dangers
> among false brethren;"**

Galatians 1:6 -9 states:

> **"I am amazed that you are so quickly deserting Him who
> called you by the grace of Christ, for a different gospel;
> which is really not another; only there are some who are
> disturbing you and want to distort the gospel of Christ.
> But even if we, or an angel from heaven, should preach
> to you a gospel contrary to what we have preached to
> you, he is to be accursed! As we have said before, so I
> say again now, if any man is preaching to you a gospel
> contrary to what you received, he is to be accursed!**

When the truth that Jesus Christ is the only way to God is challenged with "all roads lead to God," we can see why churches are in such a state of disorder! These false gospels are being injected into the churches. When the confrontation of sin is not taught but instead challenged by those who refuse to explain repentance as necessary for salvation, Satan is placing lies into the churches. When a church teaches there is no cost in following Jesus, we have a group of people who think they are saved but have no idea what giving up their life really means. These are tactics Satan uses that we as true Christians need to take a stand against.

Let's get back to our list in 2 Timothy. Hopefully, we have established a shocking truth – many people claim to know Christ but have no idea what that means. Remember, this list is from people who have "a form of godliness."

Here is the list broken down from 2 Timothy 3:1-5. These

would be considered what "fruit" would NOT be!

1. Lovers of self. Are you the most important person in your own life? Do you want your way without regard for others? We see this a lot in the marriages around us. We see women refusing to have sex with their husbands, a clearly unbiblical concept. We see women disrespecting their husbands in front of others; we see woman spending money and then lying to cover this up. Why? They are lovers of themselves. We see men telling their wives what to do all the time without regard to their feelings because they feel they are the "boss" of the marriage. They want what "they" want for dinner, they want sex when "they" want it, or they refuse to understand that being the head of the household means they are a "servant leader" in their family. What is the problem here? *Lovers of themselves.*

As you stay abiding in Christ, He will produce in you the fruit of love and kindness for others. Your life will be about pleasing others -your husband, your wife, your children – rather than yourself. If you have any of the traits above, please go before the Lord and ask Him to change you from caring only about yourself to caring about the needs of those around you.

1 Corinthians 10:24:

"Let no one seek his own good, but that of his neighbor."

Philippians 2:3-4:

"Do nothing from selfishness or empty conceit, but with humility of mind regard one another as more important than yourselves; do not merely look out for your own personal interests, but also for the interests of others."

1 Corinthians 13:5:

"(love) does not act unbecomingly; it does not seek its own, is not provoked, does not take into account a wrong suffered,"

2. *Lovers of money.* What is your view of money? Do you want to make more and more in order to get more material possessions? Do you look at money as if "you" earned it and "you" can spend it on anything "you" want? The Bible never says money is a bad thing- it does say the "love" of money is. If this is a problem for you, pray that God opens your eyes to see His view of money; money is a tool and a blessing to be used to help others come to know Christ. If God has blessed you financially and your normal thought process is to give God a little and keep most for yourself, ask God to help you truly understand you have the things you do because HE gave them to you.

Matthew 6:24 says, **"No one can serve two masters. Either he will hate the one and love the other, or he will be devoted to the one and despise the other. _You cannot serve both God and money"._** (Emphasis ours)

1 Timothy 6:10 says, **_"For the love of money_ is a root of all sorts of evil, and some by longing for it have wandered away from the faith and pierced themselves with many griefs."** (Emphasis ours)

1 Peter 5:2 says, **"Be shepherds of God's flock that is under your care, serving as overseers—not because you must, but because you are willing, as God wants you to be; _not greedy for money,_ but eager to serve;"** (NIV, emphasis ours)
Deuteronomy 8:18 says, **"But remember the Lord your God, _for it is he who gives you the ability to produce wealth,_**

and so confirms his covenant, which he swore to your forefathers, as it is today." (NIV, emphasis ours)

Remember, all you have is a gift from God. Where you spend your money determines what is in your heart. God has given you a job and an income and you are now to be a good steward of the money HE has entrusted to you. Someone once said you can tell how serious a person is about his relationship to God by looking at their calendar and their checkbook.

*3. **Boastful.*** Are you proud of what you have accomplished in your life? Do you tell people how much money you make, how great your kids are, how expensive your things are? Do you show off your new car or new boat?

If so, please understand that God is the giver of all gifts in life. Your job, your children, your worldly possessions are all from Him. Pray that God would replace your boastfulness with thanksgiving for what He has done for you and make sure your friends and neighbors know you only have the things you do because of God's grace and mercy.

Psalm 34:2:

> **"My soul will boast in the Lord; let the afflicted hear and rejoice."**

Psalm 44:8:

> **"In God we have boasted all day long, and we will give thanks to Your name forever."**

1 Corinthians 1:3:

"so that, just as it is written, 'Let him who boasts, boast in the Lord.'"

Ephesians 2:9:

"not as a result of works, so that no one may boast."

4. Pride. Are you self absorbed with yourself? Do you always think you are the smartest, the best, and always right? Pride is hard to define because it seems natural for us to care about ourselves and to think highly of ourselves and our opinions. Do you know people who act as if they are never wrong; they know everything about everything, and it is their way or no way? They are not willing to play second string in life. Pride is an overly high opinion of oneself. In the book of Daniel, King Nebuchadnezzar exhibited an enormous amount of pride. He felt as though he built his kingdom and was honoring himself for it. At that moment, after Daniel warned him to exalt God instead of himself, the Bible says this is what happened to the king:

Daniel 4:28 -33:

All this happened to Nebuchadnezzar the king. "Twelve months later he was walking on the roof of the royal palace of Babylon. The king reflected and said, 'Is this not Babylon the great, which I myself have built as a royal residence by the might of my power and for the glory of my majesty?' While the word was in the king's mouth, a voice came from heaven, saying, 'King Nebuchadnezzar, to you it is declared: sovereignty has been removed from you, and you will be driven away from mankind, and your dwelling place will be with the beasts of the field. You will be given grass to eat like cattle, and seven periods of time will pass over you until you recognize that the Most High is ruler over the realm of mankind and bestows it on whomever He wishes.' Immediately the

word concerning Nebuchadnezzar was fulfilled; and he was driven away from mankind and began eating grass like cattle, and his body was drenched with the dew of heaven until his hair had grown like eagles' feathers and his nails like birds' claws.

God hates pride. He hates it when we think highly of ourselves. He hates it when we take credit for those things He bestows upon us. For seven years, King Nebuchadnezzar lived like a wild beast until this happened:

Daniel 4:34-37:
"But at the end of that period, I, Nebuchadnezzar, raised my eyes toward heaven and my reason returned to me, and I blessed the Most High and praised and honored Him who lives forever; For His dominion is an everlasting dominion, and His kingdom endures from generation to generation. All the inhabitants of the earth are accounted as nothing, but He does according to His will in the host of heaven and among the inhabitants of earth; and no one can ward off His hand or say to Him, 'What have You done?' At that time my reason returned to me. And my majesty and splendor were restored to me for the glory of my kingdom, and my counselors and my nobles began seeking me out; so I was reestablished in my sovereignty, and surpassing greatness was added to me. Now I, Nebuchadnezzar, praise, exalt and honor the King of heaven, for all His works are true and His ways just, and He is able to humble those who walk in pride."

Remember the King's final words on this; he learned from experience that when you are prideful, God is able to humble. God restored his kingdom back to him once he recognized what he had was because of God, not himself. What about us? Are we taking credit for the things in our life that God has blessed us with? A great marriage? A successful business? Smart children? Let this be a warning – God wants the glory and honor due Him for what HE has done in our life.

Proverbs 8:13:

"The fear of the Lord is to hate evil; pride and arrogance and the evil way and the perverted mouth, I hate".

Proverbs 16:18:

"Pride goes before destruction, and a haughty spirit before stumbling."

I John 2:16 :

"For all that is in the world, the lust of the flesh and the lust of the eyes and the boastful pride of life, is not from the Father, but is from the world."

5. *Abusive.* How do you treat your spouse, children, or friends? Do you say mean things to them, do you hurt their self esteem, and do you scream and yell at them? Are you a "dream killer?" Do you physically abuse anyone? Does your anger seem to take over and you react in a violent way? God can truly change your life and your abusive behavior as you abide in His Word and be in continual prayer. The first step is to recognize you have a problem and get a true biblical counselor to help you through these issues. You will need tremendous support and help from the body of Christ. Abusive speech and behavior is not the kind of fruit that is attached to the tree of Jesus!

6. *Disobedient to parents.* Do you have respect for your parents? Do you obey what they ask of you, or do you rebel? We know of someone who hadn't seen her mother for years and, as she was driving one day, she heard a pastor preach on "honoring your father and mother." She realized she was not honoring God by not honoring her mother, so she began seeing her mom. Because of this, her mother ended up becoming a Christian, and today they have a wonderful, blessed relationship.

Romans 1:30:

> **"slanderers, haters of God, insolent, arrogant, boastful, inventors of evil, *disobedient to parents,*"** (emphasis ours)

Colossians 3:20:

> **"Children, *be obedient to your parents* in all things, for this is well-pleasing to the Lord."** (emphasis ours)

Ephesians 6:1:

> **"Children, obey your parents in the Lord, for this is right."**

7. *Ungrateful.* Are you appreciative of the things you have in your life? Are you thankful to God for giving you another day of life, or do you complain about everything? Are you unhappy about the money you make (or don't make), the home you live in, the parents or children you have? Do you hate your job, your car, or your life? If ungratefulness is a part of your life, please understand what you have is a gift from God. You may not like your situation or circumstances, but God calls us to be thankful and grateful for where we are in life.

Psalm 105:1:

> **"Oh give thanks to the Lord, call upon His name; make known His deeds among the peoples."**

Colossians 3:15:

> **"Let the peace of Christ rule in your hearts, to which indeed you were called in one body; and be thankful."**

Colossians 2:7:

> **"having been firmly rooted and now being built up in Him and established in your faith, just as you were instructed, and overflowing with gratitude."**

Philippians 4:6:

> **"Be anxious for nothing, but in everything by prayer and supplication with thanksgiving let your requests be made known to God."**

Remember, God says we are to pray about everything with thanksgiving. Maybe you should start by thanking God for the things you feel ungrateful about in your life. Thank Him for the lack of money, the wayward child, or the unsaved spouse. Thank Him for the job you hate, the house that is too small, and the people you don't get along with in your life. When you realize that as a Christian God has placed you where you are for a purpose, then you can be grateful. Romans 8:28 says, **"And we know that in all things God works for the good of those who love him, who have been called according to his purpose."** As a Christian God promises He will work out in your life the things that seem so hopeless; He will work it out for His purpose.

8. ***Unholy.*** Holiness means being "set apart" from evil. It

carries with it the idea that as we grow in our relationship with Christ, we don't want to live in the sins of the past. Are you still living a lifestyle that contradicts holy living? God calls us be holy as He is holy. Can you say that about yourself, or do you find your life reflecting unholy behaviors?

2 Peter 3:11:

> **"Since all these things are to be destroyed in this way, what sort of people ought you to be in holy conduct and godliness…"**

Romans 12:1:

> **"Therefore I urge you, brethren, by the mercies of God, to present your bodies a living and holy sacrifice, acceptable to God, which is your spiritual service of worship."**

2 Timothy 1:9:

> **"who has saved us and called us with a holy calling, not according to our works, but according to His own purpose and grace which was granted us in Christ Jesus from all eternity,"**

9. *Without love.* How do you treat people? Do you generally have a love for most people, or is your life filled with hatred or bitterness towards others? Do you love those who are hard to love? Remember, it is easy to love the lovable, but what about those who are not nice to us? What about an out of control boss or spouse? Can you still love them?

1 Peter 1:22:

> **"Since you have in obedience to the truth purified your**

souls for a sincere love of the brethren, fervently love one another from the heart,"

1 Peter 4:8:

"**Above all, keep fervent in your love for one another, because love covers a multitude of sins.**"

1 John 3:10-11:

"**By this the children of God and the children of the devil are obvious: anyone who does not practice righteousness is not of God, nor the one who does not love his brother. For this is the message which you have heard from the beginning, that we should love one another;**"

1 John 4:7-8:

"**Beloved, let us love one another, for love is from God; and everyone who loves is born of God and knows God. The one who does not love does not know God, for God is love.**"

James 2:8:

"**If, however, you are fulfilling the royal law according to the Scripture, "You shall love your neighbor as yourself," you are doing well.**"

10. Unforgiving. Have you gotten over past hurts? Has someone said something to you or done something to you that you can't seem to forgive and forget? Maybe a child has hurt you by leaving home without saying "thank you," maybe your spouse has left you for someone else and now you are single and bitter, or maybe your parents or someone you knew hurt you mentally or physically, and you can't seem to forgive them. Forgiveness is tough; this is something God alone can produce in your life. Face it, confess it, and move on in your life. The Bible says in Philippians 3:13-14, **"Brethren, I do not regard myself as having laid hold of it yet; but one thing I do: forgetting what lies behind and reaching forward to what lies ahead, I press on toward the goal for the prize of the upward call of God in Christ Jesus."**

Whatever has happened in your life that has led to your unforgiving attitude, remember nothing has happened in your past that God did not "cause" or "allow" for His purposes. Use your past hurts and pains to help others who are going through the same thing. You can forgive those who have hurt you, especially when you realize that a Sovereign God has allowed the problem in your life. You can move on knowing that He is moving you in a different direction, and you can have peace and comfort knowing nothing came into your life without first passing through His loving and wise hands.

Colossians 3:13:

> **"bearing with one another, and forgiving each other, whoever has a complaint against anyone; just as the Lord forgave you, so also should you."**

Matthew 18:21-22:

> **"Then Peter came and said to Him, "Lord, how often shall my brother sin against me and I forgive him? Up to seven times?" Jesus said to him, "I do not say to you, up to seven times, but up to seventy times seven."**

11. Slanderous. What do you say about others behind their backs? Do you gossip about others, slander their name or their reputation? When we begin to take into consideration that each

Christian is at a different spiritual level, we can be more forgiving and less slanderous. We were in a meeting once where a fellow believer was being slandered. A few weeks later, we were talking with someone who had been in that same meeting and, forgetting we had heard the same thing, this man proceeded to repeat what he had heard. The problem was we knew the slandered man and we knew what was said was not true. The issue was that the man being slandered had not grown spiritually as fast as others had grown and, therefore, he didn't act as he should. We need to understand that some people do not act as they should because of lack of knowledge of God's Word. Maybe they are new believers or maybe God has not dealt in their life in a certain area yet. When we understand this, we can quit talking about them behind their backs. We can be the ones encouraging others to give people grace and mercy instead of gossip and slander.

Titus 3:2:

"to slander no one, to be peaceable and considerate, and to show true humility toward all men."

Romans 1:30:

"slanderers, God-haters, insolent, arrogant and boastful; they invent ways of doing evil; they disobey their parents;"

1 Corinthians 6:10:

"nor thieves nor the greedy nor drunkards nor slanderers nor swindlers will inherit the kingdom of God"

Leviticus 19:16:

"Do not go about spreading slander among your people. Do not do anything that endangers your neighbor's

life. I am the Lord."

12. __Self control.__ Do you have self control over things like alcohol, drugs, pornography or gambling? How about self-control over things like eating (for Lisa, that would be chocolate chip cookies, and for Rob, that would be ice cream), gossip, or bad language? All of these are problems we need to come to terms with and allow God to change us from the inside out. Ask God to give you the ability to control your desires and help you desire the things of God instead of actions that you have no control over in your life.

2 Peter 1:6:

> **"and to knowledge, self-control; and to self-control, perseverance; and to perseverance, godliness;"**

1 Corinthians 7:5:

> **"Do not deprive each other except by mutual consent and for a time, so that you may devote yourselves to prayer. Then come together again so that Satan will not tempt you because of your lack of self-control."**

1 Timothy 3:2:

> **"Now the overseer must be above reproach, the husband of but one wife, temperate, self-controlled, respectable, hospitable, able to teach,"**

Titus 1:8:

> **"Rather he must be hospitable, one who loves what is good, who is self-controlled, upright, holy and disciplined."**

Titus 2:12:

> **"instructing us to deny ungodliness and worldly desires**

and to live sensibly, righteously and godly in the present age,"

13. Brutal, not lovers of good, treacherous, rash, conceited. People with these traits are harsh, not caring for anything of good repute, but caring only for the bad in life. These are mean and selfish characteristics Satan and the world love to produce. These need to be replaced with kindness and goodness that can only come from the Holy Spirit working in our lives.

14. Lovers of pleasure rather than lovers of God. Does your lifestyle, your hobbies, and your work reflect a love for God? Do you care more for the pleasures of life – the parties, the sports events, and the theatre, more than you do the things of God?

Proverbs 21:17:
"He who loves pleasure will become poor; whoever loves wine and oil will never be rich."

Hebrews 11:25:
"He chose to be mistreated along with the people of God rather than to enjoy the pleasures of sin for a short time."

The point in this section is to question yourself. What is your life producing? Perhaps you are a new believer, and you see for the first time how you have been behaving is not conducive to being a "new creature in Christ." The hope here is that as you attach yourself to Christ and abide in His Word, these things will be worked out of your life, not just passively ignored.

When a person first becomes a Christian, he begins what is called the "sanctification process," which in simple terms means the "growing process." Most people do not grow up in one day; it takes years and years to grow up physically; the same holds true spiritually. Remember, all Christians continue to go through this process. What God worked out in your life years ago might not be what He is working out in someone else at the moment. We cannot judge where a person is in his or her walk with God, but we can look at ourselves. Do you see things in the list above that concern you? If so, confess these things to God, turn from these behaviors, and pray that God would change you from the inside out. Remember, He is working out the bad fruit and replacing it with true, real fruit that can only be obtained by being attached to Him.

CHAPTER 6

WHAT DOES TRUE FRUIT LOOK LIKE?

Now that we have taken a look at what fruit is "not," we can begin on the list that shows what fruit "is." Take the time as you read this list to see if true fruit is what your life is producing. One day during Bible study, I (Lisa) had someone ask me, "What if I am only producing certain fruit and not others? Does that mean I'm not a Christian?" Great questions, ones that we will feel tension about for most of our lives. Here is what we need to remember: Philippians 1:6 says, **"For I am confident of this very thing, that He who began a good work in you will perfect it until the day of Christ Jesus."**

The first day you become a Christian is the first day God has begun a good work in you. For most of us, He doesn't remove all the bad things at once. It takes a lifetime to work out all the "bad" fruit and replace it with the "good" fruit. As we read His Word, we begin to see what the bad things are in our life: the pride, the bad attitudes, the habits we have formed over all the years we were not Christians. When we see these things, instead of ignoring them and continuing on, we pray and ask God to change us. We pray He will replace the ugliness in our lives with the good fruit He produces by being attached to Him.

Amazingly, He changes us. As we look back over our lives, we begin to see attitudes and actions we once had that are not there anymore. That is how it happens. We open the Bible, read it, and the Holy Spirit uses the Word of God to change our lives.

How can a man who was a drunk most of his life never pick up a drink again? How can a person who hated God all his life now be a true and devoted follower of Jesus? How can a marriage that was falling apart now be restored and better now than ever? How can a person who was possessive and jealous most of his life now have a peace and contentment about him? How can someone who used to swear all the time now be repulsed by hearing bad language?

Only God can do this. Only God can replace the things of your past with wonderful things for your future. How does this happen? It happens supernaturally and miraculously. We cannot do this on our own. These changes can only happen by the Holy Spirit who resides in our lives, who changes us as we read His Word. We cannot stress this enough, so we will repeat this again. The Holy Spirit changes our lives when we read the Bible. This is a simple equation – as we read the Bible, the Holy Spirit convicts us of things that need to be changed. This cannot happen if we are not reading His Word. Reading the Bible has to become the most important thing in our lives if we want to change.

The problem comes when we have an anger problem and it doesn't immediately go away. The problem comes when we can't produce love for someone we naturally don't like. We begin to doubt and question if we truly are Christians. Remember what we said before – RELAX. Continue to abide (or remain) in Christ. He promises He will produce these things in your life. Continue to come before the Lord with the things in your life you know He doesn't like. HE will change you, YOU cannot change yourself. We will start with the verses from Galatians 5:22-23:

"But the fruit of the Spirit is love, joy, peace, patience, kindness, goodness, faithfulness, gentleness and self-control. Against such things there is no law."

As we break these verses apart, take a look at your own life and see if these things are being produced in you. We will take these traits one at a time just as we did with "What Fruit is Not." If you come across something that doesn't look like your life, confess it to God and ask Him to produce that particular fruit in your life. The first fruit we will discuss is love.

CHAPTER 7

LOVE

Love is so hard to explain because most people believe it is a feeling. If you got married it was because you fell "in love." Most divorces happen because people fall "out of love." If you turn on the television or watch movies, you will see the world's definition of love. You will notice it usually has something to do with a feeling and not a commitment. The Bible spends a great deal of time explaining what the biblical definition of love is in 1 Corinthians 13. Let's see what it has to say.

1 Corinthians 13:4 -7 (NIV):

"Love is patient, love is kind. It does not envy, it does not boast, it is not proud. It is not rude, it is not self-seeking, it is not easily angered, it keeps no record of wrongs. Love does not delight in evil but rejoices with the truth. It always protects, always trusts, always hopes, always perseveres."

a. ***Are you patient with those around you?*** Love says you will be. What about your husband, wife, children, or parents? How about the people in your office? What happens when someone annoys you? What is your reaction? When you love someone, it means you will be patient with them.

1 Thessalonians 5:14:

> **"We urge you, brethren, admonish the unruly, encourage the fainthearted, help the weak, be patient with every one."**

2 Corinthians 6:4 (NKJV):

> **"But in all things we commend ourselves as ministers of God: in much patience, in tribulations, in needs, in distresses,"**

b. ***Are you kind to those around you?*** Love says you will be. What happens when you don't get your own way? Do you care more for the needs of those around you than for yourself? When you love someone it means you are kind to them. Do you do things for others even if you don't always "feel" like it? Do you visit someone in the hospital when it is inconvenient? Do you watch your children for a day so you can give your spouse a break even if it means you will miss the golf game or nail appointment? Kindness tells someone you truly love them regardless of your own personal wants and needs.

Colossians 3:12:

> **"So, as those who have been chosen of God, holy and beloved, put on a heart of compassion, kindness, humility, gentleness and patience;"**

Proverbs 31:26:

> **"She opens her mouth in wisdom, and the teaching of kindness is on her tongue."**

c. ***Are you envious of those around you?*** When you love someone, you won't be. Maybe they have a bigger home or a nicer spouse. Maybe they have more money than you, and you feel jealous and envious. Love in action says that it doesn't matter if someone has something you don't. Love says you are happy for those that have what you don't.

James 3:16 (NIV):

"For where you have envy and selfish ambition, there you find disorder and every evil practice."

1 Peter 2:1-2:

"Therefore, putting aside all malice and all deceit and hypocrisy and envy and all slander, like newborn babies, long for the pure milk of the word, so that by it you may grow in respect to salvation,"

d. ***Do you boast about the blessings you have in your life?*** Great kids? Great spouse? Great job? What about a new home, a new boat, or a new car? Love never boasts about these things. When you love someone, you cannot boast about these things because you know all things are gifts from God to you. You don't deserve them, but He has given them to you anyway, therefore, boasting is never an option. When you flaunt what you have in front of others, that is not love.

Psalm 44:8:

"In God we have boasted all day long, and we will give thanks to Your name forever."

Psalm 34:2:

"My soul will make its boast in the Lord; the humble will hear it and rejoice."

e. ***Are you proud?*** Pride is an over-exaggerated opinion of yourself. When pride raises its ugly head, you act as if that the world should revolve around you and your opinions. Do you let others share their feelings and opinions or do you always have to be right? Love lets others know they are important, their thoughts matter greatly to you, and you have a humble, apologetic heart when you know you are wrong. That is love in action.

Proverbs 13:10 (NIV):

"Pride only breeds quarrels, but wisdom is found in those who take advice."

Proverbs 28:25 (NIV):

"He who is of a proud heart stirs up strife, but he who trusts in the Lord will be prospered."

f. ***Are you rude?*** If you love someone, you won't be. Do you think you have a higher status than someone else, and, therefore, you respond with a sharp, condescending attitude toward them? How do you treat waitresses in the restaurants or store clerks at the mall? Love is not rude. It never treats others as if they are less of a person. Love never has a demeaning attitude toward others.

g. ***Are you self-seeking?*** When you love someone, you're not. Many marriages could be saved if each person would realize love means thinking of and doing for the other person before themselves. Love says to another person that their needs and wants are more important than your own.

Philippians 2:21:

"For they all seek after their own interests, not those of Christ Jesus."

2 Corinthians 5:15:

"and He died for all, so that they who live might no longer live for themselves, but for Him who died and rose again on their behalf."

h. ***Do you get mad easily?*** If you love someone, you won't. What happens when your time or space are invaded? Maybe your kids didn't do something you asked or your wife forgot to pick up the laundry. What is your response? Do you scream and yell and get mad? Love says it's okay and stays calm. Love says you care more for the other person regardless of the circumstances.

Proverbs 15:1:

"A gentle answer turns away wrath, but a harsh word stirs up anger."

Proverbs 14:29:

"He who is slow to anger has great understanding, but he who is quick-tempered exalts folly."

Ecclesiastes 7:9:

"Do not be eager in your heart to be angry, for anger resides in the bosom of fools."

i. ***Do you remember and keep a record of people who have hurt you?*** If you love someone, you won't. Do you hold grudges against those who treated you poorly in the past? When you love someone, you forgive them. When you love someone, you move on, forgetting what happened in the past and reaching forward to the future.

Philippians 3:13:

"Brethren, I do not regard myself as having laid hold of

it yet; but one thing I do: forgetting what lies behind and reaching forward to what lies ahead,"

As you can see from this long list about love, it isn't so much a feeling as it is a commitment and a choice. Feelings come and go, but when you love someone, you will do all these things regardless of a feeling. The world has done a great disservice to this word. Love is an action; it displays qualities like patience and kindness. Nowhere do we see we have to feel it in order to do it.

Remember this: Jesus demonstrated His love for us by dying on a cross. That was an action, not a feeling.

Romans 5:8:

"But God demonstrates His own love toward us, in that while we were yet sinners, Christ died for us."

CHAPTER 8

JOY

The next fruit of the Spirit that is produced in our life is joy. This is a feeling of happiness or pleasure. The problem with the world's view of joy is that it is dependent on something pleasurable happening to us or around us. But the Bible expresses joy to be something we can have regardless of good times or bad times. Look at what the Bible says about joy:

Habakkuk 3:17-18:

"Though the fig tree should not blossom and there be no fruit on the vines, though the yield of the olive should fail and the fields produce no food, though the flock should be cut off from the fold and there be no cattle in the stalls, yet I will exult in the Lord, I will rejoice in the God of my salvation."

Habakkuk learned that God was going to use an evil nation to discipline the nation of Israel. This was a tough time for him, and he questioned what God was doing, but by the end of the book of Habakkuk, this was his conclusion: he would be joyful in God even though there was no food and his world was falling apart. He knew he could be joyful because he knew the God who controlled these events. He realized God had purposes beyond what he could imagine.

That is how God wants us to live. As we stay attached to Him, learning and growing daily in His Word, we can be joyful when the world seems to be falling apart. If Habakkuk had not known God and His ways, he would have fallen apart like most people who don't know Christ. There is hope in Christ, hope that He works all things for good, and that alone is enough to be joyful.

Psalm 16:8-9:

"I have set the Lord continually before me; because He is at my right hand, I will not be shaken. Therefore my heart is glad and my glory rejoices; my flesh also will dwell securely."

James 1:2-3:

"Consider it all joy, my brethren, when you encounter various trials, knowing that the testing of your faith produces endurance."

As you can see from this verse, a Christian can be joyful even when bad things come into our lives. The reason we can be joyful is because we know God is in control of all our circumstances. He brings trials and hardships in order to test our faith and bring perseverance. He brings trials and hardships into our lives in order to show us how to trust Him with our lives. That is why we can have joy.

We can be confident everything that comes into our life has been filtered through the hands of our loving God who works all things out in our lives for good. We can be joyful in life because we are His. The difference between what the world tells us and what

God tells us is that the world produces joy when things are going great, but the Bible says that the Holy Spirit will fill us with joy regardless if things are going great or not. This is a fruit that can only be produced by God in our lives.

CHAPTER 9

PEACE

Webster's Dictionary says that to be peaceful means you are undisturbed by strife or turmoil. Is that very easy to have in this day and age? What about war, earthquakes, and famine? What about cancer, heart problems, and high blood pressure? What about wayward children, drugs, and alcohol in the schools? How can I have peace when all of these frightening things are going on around me? Look what the Bible says about peace.

Isaiah 45:7:

"The One forming light and creating darkness, causing well-being and creating calamity; I am the Lord who does all these."

What an amazing verse! God takes full responsibility for creating calamity! When I know this, I can have peace. I can know for certain He is completely in control of all things that go on in this world. When war or famine strikes, I know the God I have put my trust in is in complete control. I can rest assured He is working all things to an end that glorifies Him the most.

What if I get cancer? I can be at total peace He is in control. What if He is using cancer to show those around me I truly trust in God? What if cancer gives me more opportunities to share the gospel? What if this sickness gives me a bigger platform to show the grace and mercy of God?

When I look at all things in life coming directly from the hand of God, then I can have peace. As a child of God, I know He only has good purposes in mind for me and those I come in contact with. Is cancer worth it if one person comes to know Christ because of it? We have to start looking at life from an eternal point of view and not a worldly point of view. The world would say it is hopeless - God would say He is in complete control and that is why peace is a fruit of the Spirit. How can I have peace in the midst of heartache? How can I have peace when my world seems to be falling apart? Without the Holy Spirit living in me producing this peace, it won't happen. This peace is only a product of a life that abides in Christ. The more I read His Word, the more I know the God I have placed my faith in and the more peace I have.

Psalm 147:14:

"He makes peace in your borders; He satisfies you with the finest of the wheat."

Philippians 4:7:

"And the peace of God, which surpasses all comprehension, will guard your hearts and your minds in Christ Jesus."

John 14:27:

"Peace I leave with you, My peace I give to you; not as the world gives do I give to you. Let not your heart be

troubled, neither let it be afraid."

John 16:33:

"These things I have spoken to you, so that in Me you may have peace. In the world you have tribulation, but take courage; I have overcome the world."

CHAPTER 10

PATIENCE

We have a friend who was totally frustrated one day because she was stuck in the line at McDonalds for five minutes. That seemed like an eternity – she felt she should have been out of there in two. We laughed about it later because she said she realized she just got an entire meal for her family in 5 minutes and yet that wasn't quite good enough! Isn't that just like the world we live in today? Everything has to be done quickly, or we lose our patience.

We have this problem, too. If someone needs a job and we pray for this and it doesn't happen in a day – we are frustrated. If we are praying for a loved one's salvation and it doesn't happen in a week – we are frustrated. If a sickness lasts too long, if a wayward child stays away to long, or if we have to wait too long in a store – we are frustrated. What we need is a good dose of something that seems hard to come by these days: patience.

A great definition of patience is "enduring something disagreeable or difficult without complaint." (Merriam Webster's Collegiate Thesaurus). What a great definition. Patience is not grumbling when we encounter difficulty. Patience is persevering and enduring through hard times without complaining. The more we talk about patience, the more we realize we don't have much of it. The world says things have to happen "now" and yet God says He does things on His own timing. That is why this fruit is grown only by being attached to Jesus. The more we learn His ways, the more patience we can have. This trait is not something we can conjure up on our own – we know, we have tried.

We have tried to be patient when someone is running late. We usually honk the horn a few hundred times to get their attention. We have tried to be patient when we need a business deal to go through – but instead we worry and fret. We have tried to be patient when we see our children going through tough times – but we forget God allows our children to go through hard times to grow in Him. We can't do this "patience thing" on our own because we will always fall short. Why? Because, unless we have a high, biblical view of God, we will not have the ability to be patient.

Reading God's Word and praying are key components to patience. When we understand God allows bad things to happen for a purpose, we can be patient. When we understand His timing is always perfect, we can be patient. If we pray for the salvation of someone close to us, we can be patient because we know God who is in control of salvation. When our children do things that go against what we have taught them, we can be patient, knowing God is working these things out in their lives. When someone we know is very ill and we pray for healing and it doesn't happen right away, we can be patient because we know God's timing is always perfect.

Once again, the key to this fruit is being attached to Christ. We can only produce the fruit of patience when we begin to understand who God is and that His ways are always higher than ours. Do we always understand or agree with how God does things? No, but we can patiently wait for His answers because we know Him.

Here are two excerpts from a book called Encyclopedia of 7700 *Illustrations.*

3461 To Test A Missionary Candidate

At 3:00 A.M. one cold morning a missionary candidate walked into an office for a scheduled interview with the examiner of a mission board. He waited until 8:00 A.M. when the examiner arrived.

The examiner said, "Let us begin. First, please spell baker."

"B-a-k-e-r," the young man spelled.

"Very good. Now, let's see what you know about figures. How much is twice two?"

"Four," replied the applicant.

"Very good," the examiner said. "I'll recommend to the board tomorrow that you be appointed. You have passed the test."

At the board meeting the examiner spoke highly of the applicant and said, "He has all the qualifications of a missionary. Let me explain.

"First, I tested him on self-denial. I told him to be at my house at three in the morning. He left a warm bed and came out in the cold without a word of complaint.

"Second, I tried him out on punctuality. He appeared on time.

"Third, I examined him on patience. I made him wait five hours to see me, after telling him to come at three.

"Fourth, I tested him on temper. He failed to show any sign of it; he didn't even question my delay.

"Fifth, I tried his humility. I asked him questions that a small child could answer, and he showed no offense. He meets the requirements and will make the missionary we need."

This man clearly showed fruit. He was humble, he wasn't annoyed easily, he wasn't proud; he was gentle and he exhibited an enormous amount of patience. I'm not so sure we could have passed the test! Here is another example:

3670 This Mother Prayed 60 Years

Dr. John F. Walvoord, in the chapel of Dallas Theological Seminary, one day told of a mother who prayed for her son for 60 years to be saved. One week before her death, the mother received a long-distance call from her son saying that he was saved.

Could you imagine praying for someone for 60 years? Could you imagine the amount of patience and trust that would take? We had a woman work in our office many years ago, and I (Lisa) put her on my prayer list asking God to save her. After about a year of no change or desire, I quit praying. How sad for this woman that my patience to pray for her ran out.

Grow in your relationship with Christ so this fruit can be evidenced in your life. The more we are attached to Him, the more He can give us the inner strength to wait patiently for His timing.

Psalm 40:1:

"I waited patiently for the Lord; and He inclined to me and heard my cry."

Romans 12:12 (NIV):

"Be joyful in hope, patient in affliction, faithful in prayer."

Psalm 37:7:

"Rest in the Lord and wait patiently for Him; do not fret because of him who prospers in his way, because of the

man who carries out wicked schemes."

James 1:3 (NIV):

"knowing that the testing of your faith produces patience."

CHAPTER 11

KINDNESS

Webster's Dictionary defines kind as "friendly, generous, or warm-hearted in nature, humane, considerate, forbearing, and tolerant." This is easy to do for the people we like, but what about those who try to hurt us? What about the people who are mean to us or talk bad about us behind our backs? How can we possibly be kind to someone who is out to hurt us?

This can only happen by the work of the Holy Spirit. Only He can give us what it takes to be kind to those we feel don't deserve kindness. This is what the Bible says about being kind.

Matthew 5:43 -48

"You have heard that it was said, 'You shall love your neighbor and hate your enemy.' But I say to you, love your enemies, bless those who curse you, do good to those who hate you, and pray for those who spitefully use you and persecute you, that you may be sons of your Father in heaven; for He makes His sun rise on the evil and on the good, and sends rain on the just and on the unjust. For if you love those who love you, what reward have you? Do

not even the tax collectors do the same? And if you greet your brethren only, what do you do more than others? Do not even the tax collectors do so? Therefore you shall be perfect, just as your Father in heaven is perfect."

Here is what Jesus has to say:

1. Love your enemies
2. Bless those that curse you
3. Do good to those who hate you
4. Pray for those who spitefully use you and persecute you.

How hard is this to do?! Jesus has made it clear it doesn't matter how someone treats us, it only matters what our response is to them. When someone says something behind your back to hurt you, what is your response? Do you get angry, strike back, and try to get back at them? Guess what the Bible says we have to do? Pray for them, bless them, and be kind to them. That cannot happen on our own. That has to come from a relationship with Jesus as we stay attached to Him.

Look at what Proverbs 25:21-22 says:

"If your enemy is hungry, give him food to eat; and if he is thirsty, give him water to drink; for you will heap burning coals on his head, and the Lord will reward you."

In God's economy, He says by doing kind things to those who hurt you, you will be rewarded. Maybe not today or tomorrow, maybe not even in this life, but He does promise you will be rewarded. He says doing a kind thing for your enemies is like heaping coals of fire on their head.

We have come to understand that being unkind in our words and actions can be a bad habit. I (Lisa) was talking to a girl one day who said she never had anything nice to say to her husband. It was easier to just snap at him and say something mean rather than to talk with kind words. It had become a bad habit. When she realized it, she changed. She started meeting her husband at the door, speaking kind words to him. When he said something she didn't like, instead of giving him an ugly look, she acted with kindness. Kindness works. As a Christian, this is a fruit that God commands of us.

Once again, this can only happen when you are a true believer, when you have the life of the Holy Spirit flowing through you and you are obeying His Word. Try this out in your own life. Put into practice praying for those who hurt you and being kind to those who use you. You will be blessed beyond measure and you will begin to realize that kindness is something you can do. Ask God to show you the unkind things you do and the unkind words you say. Ask Him to show you these things and by the power of the Holy Spirit living within you, ask Him to change you from the inside out.

Colossians 3:12:

"So, as those who have been chosen of God, holy and beloved, put on a heart of compassion, kindness, humility, gentleness and patience;"

Proverbs 31:26:

"She opens her mouth in wisdom, and the teaching of kindness is on her tongue."

Job 6:14:

"For the despairing man there should be kindness from his friend; so that he does not forsake the fear of the Almighty."

Ephesians 4:31-32:

> **"Let all bitterness and wrath and anger and clamor and slander be put away from you, along with all malice. Be kind to one another, tender-hearted, forgiving each other, just as God in Christ also has forgiven you."**

CHAPTER 12

GOODNESS

A friend of ours had gone to a big, religious convention with a group of women who claimed to live righteous, moral lives. After the convention was over, they went to a scrap book store where the store was handing out free gift bags – one per person. These women were taking handfuls and walking out the door. They rationalized that the store wouldn't mind – they were giving these bags away anyway. Trying to figure out the meaning of goodness, this story came to our mind.

Goodness means to be morally excellent. Words that would mean the same would be things like honesty, integrity, uprightness, and virtue. Basically, it means to do the right thing. Isn't it easy in this world to compromise? Isn't it easy to cheat just a little on your taxes? Isn't it easy to let someone under charge you at the store and never say anything? Integrity and goodness means holding firm to the conviction of doing the right thing – regardless if it costs you something.

Proverbs 10:9:
   "He who walks in integrity walks securely, but he who

perverts his ways will be found out."

When Rob turned 50, the kids and I decided to give him a surprise party. In order to keep it a surprise, we had to lie about everything. When we were looking for a band, we had to tell Rob we were at the grocery store. When we were with the caterers, we had to tell him we were at the mall. We were so glad when the party was over. Lying was exhausting. It was all done in order to keep a secret, (which actually was the biggest surprise of his life), but I was shocked at how tired I was trying to keep the lies straight.

The Bible says that a person who lives a good, honest lifestyle with integrity will walk securely. He is secure because he never has to look over his shoulder wondering if he will be found out.

Psalm 26:1:
> **"Vindicate me, O Lord, for I have walked in my
> integrity, and I have trusted in the Lord without wavering."**

When we live a life filled with goodness, we can trust the Lord will take care of us. If we're honest on our income taxes, God will provide for us. If we refuse to lie for our boss, God will provide for us.

Job is a perfect example of what goodness is. He was a righteous, upright man and stayed that way even when everything was taken from him.

Job 2:3:
> **"The Lord said to Satan, "Have you considered My
> servant Job? For there is no one like him on the earth,
> a blameless and upright man fearing God and turning
> away from evil. And he still holds fast his integrity,**

although you incited Me against him to ruin him without cause."

Job was upright because he feared God, which means he had a high, respectful view of God. He wanted to do good because He didn't want to offend a holy God. Job's wife wasn't much help in the situation. This is what she said in Job 2:9:

"Then his wife said to him, "Do you still hold fast to your integrity? Curse God and die!"

Even his wife saw the integrity he had. At this point Job had just found out his 10 children were killed, his animals were taken away, and his servants were killed. He was also afflicted with painful boils. You can tell a lot about a person when confronted with tragedy. Do they "curse God," or do they continue living with integrity and goodness? Job was the perfect example of righteous living without compromise. What about you? Can you still be honest even if it means you might lose your job? Can you still tell the truth even if it means trouble? Can you still be honest on your income taxes even if it means you have to pay more?

Once again this fruit can only be obtained by being attached to Christ. He gives the ability to make the right decisions – even if those decisions hurt. After everything Job had been through, in the end the Bible says, "the Lord blessed the latter days of Job more than his beginning." God blesses goodness, honesty and integrity. If you struggle in this area, go before the Lord and ask Him to help you make the right decisions in your life.

Psalm 41:12:
"As for me, You uphold me in my integrity, and You set

me in Your presence forever."

Proverbs 20:7:

"A righteous man who walks in his integrity— how blessed are his sons after him."

CHAPTER 13

FAITHFULNESS

The world we live in doesn't seem to grasp the concept of faithfulness. With so many divorces, so many adulterous affairs, so many friendships breaking apart, and so many business deals going south, it's no wonder faithfulness is a hot commodity.

Faithfulness looks like this:

I will stay faithful to you in my marriage regardless of how I feel.

I will keep what you tell me in confidence because you are my friend.

I will stay by your side even when hard times hit.

I will never bad mouth you to anyone.

I will be here for you in your sickness.

I will stay in this business deal even if I lose money because we are in this together.

Faithfulness is hard to come by today. People want the easy way out of a marriage, a friendship or a business. Many do not know what it means to be loyal and supportive when times are bad.

In a world that says "it's all about me," it is hard to be faithful.

Proverbs 20:6 says:

"Many a man proclaims his own loyalty, but who can find a trustworthy man?"

Even Solomon, the wisest man to ever live, understood this. Faithfulness is hard to find. What about us? What can we do to live a faithful life to our spouses, children, and friends? First of all, understanding this is a fruit of the Spirit should help us realize how important faithfulness is for a Christian to have. When the world says run, walk away from the problem and think only of yourself, the Bible counteracts with "Christians don't do that." He wants His children to be characterized by faithfulness. He wants us to be known by this fruit. We don't run when our marriage seems hopeless. We don't tell others what is told to us in confidence. We are loyal to others and to people we have given our word to.

This is produced by abiding in Christ. This is produced by reading His Word. We need to see how important this trait is in a Christian.

3 John 5:

"Beloved, you are acting faithfully in whatever you accomplish for the brethren, and especially when they are strangers;"

Proverbs 11:13:

"He who goes about as a talebearer reveals secrets, but he who is trustworthy conceals a matter."

Psalm 31:23:

"O love the Lord, all you His godly ones! The Lord reserves the faithful and fully recompenses the proud doer"

In the book of Daniel in the Old Testament, Daniel was faithful all of his life to God. Because of this, when the governors and officials tried to find fault with him, they couldn't. He stood for God regardless of the cost of his position. He refused to compromise his faith. He spoke the truth to kings regardless if it cost him his life. He refused to bow down to idols because of his faithfulness to his God. Daniel is a life we should study so we can see that, even through the bad times, we still can exhibit this quality.

Daniel 6:4-6:

"Then the commissioners and satraps began trying to find a ground of accusation against Daniel in regard to government affairs; but they could find no ground of accusation or evidence of corruption, in as much as he was faithful, and no negligence or corruption was to be found in him. Then these men said, "We will not find any ground of accusation against this Daniel unless we find it against him with regard to the law of his God." Then these commissioners and satraps came by agreement to the king and spoke to him as follows: "King Darius, live forever!"

What an amazing way to live! They could find nothing against him at all! He was faithful to his king, he was faithful in his job, and he was faithful to his friends. This kind of lifestyle should be the norm for Christians. We should learn a very valuable lesson from Daniel. He was faithful to the end because he was faithful in the daily habit of spending time with God. He will in His faithfulness give us the power to do whatever He calls us to do, just like He did with Daniel.

Daniel 6:10:

> **"Now when Daniel knew that the document was signed, he entered his house (now in his roof chamber he had windows open toward Jerusalem); and he continued kneeling on his knees three times a day, praying and giving thanks before his God, as he had been doing previously."**

1 Thessalonians 5:24:

> **"Faithful is He who calls you, and He also will bring it to pass."**

CHAPTER 14

GENTLENESS

2 Timothy 2:24-26

"And the Lord's servant must not quarrel; instead, he must be kind to everyone, able to teach, not resentful. Those who oppose him he must gently instruct, in the hope that God will grant them repentance leading them to a knowledge of the truth, and that they will come to their senses and escape from the trap of the devil, who has taken them captive to do his will."

What an amazing verse that captures how God calls us to act, especially to those who are not Christians! When we started sharing our faith with people, it seemed easier and more spiritual (which it wasn't) to argue with people - my way is right, your way is wrong. Our voices would be raised, the tension would rise, and we would walk away looking like jerks. No wonder God put this verse in the Bible – it must have been just for us!

But that is not God's way. He wants gentleness, meekness, and humility. He wants us to use kind words and kind gestures with a gentleness about us. Jesus is the perfect example of gentleness and meekness.

1 Peter 2:21:

"To this you were called, because Christ suffered for you, leaving you an example, that you should follow in his steps. He committed no sin, and no deceit was found in his mouth. When they hurled their insults at him, he did not retaliate; when he suffered, he made no threats. Instead, he entrusted himself to him who judges justly."

True gentleness can only be produced by the Holy Spirit. True gentleness says it doesn't matter what is done to me, I don't need to retaliate. How hard is that in this day and age? We want our way, our rights should never be violated and it is our prerogative to scream and yell and tell you how we feel. Gentleness lets other people win. Gentleness means I am considerate and kind without being violent or harsh.

We find this difficult with our children. When they fall and hurt themselves (for the tenth time in ten minutes), we tend to not be filled with gentleness. Our words are more like "get up, you're fine," "stop acting like this," or "you're going right to bed when we get home." What could possibly be gentle about that! But Jesus modeled this to perfection. When being beaten or hanging on the cross, He only cared for others. He was God. He could have destroyed everyone in a second, but He didn't. He knew what His purpose was, which is what we could use as a lesson for us.

Matthew 11:29:

"Take My yoke upon you and learn from Me, for I am gentle and humble in heart, and you will find rest for your souls.

Galatians 6:1:

"Brethren, even if anyone is caught in any trespass, you who are spiritual, restore such a one in a spirit of gentleness; each one looking to yourself, so that you too will not be tempted."

Because we are Christians we have one goal in life. Live like Jesus and share Him with everyone we meet. Can we do this by being unloving and harsh? Can we do this by wanting to win theological arguments? God says it is by gentleness and humility that people will be won to Christ. This is a great lesson for us.

James 3:17:

"But the wisdom that comes from heaven is first of all pure; then peace-loving, considerate, submissive, full of mercy and good fruit, impartial and sincere."

CHAPTER 15

SELF-CONTROL

The fruit of self control is the hardest fruit for us to write about mostly because we have no self-control when it comes to chocolate chip cookies and ice cream (we have just talked ourselves into believing cookies and ice cream are gifts from God, not self control issues!). We have come to learn that self-control is a fruit that clearly has to be implemented by the Holy Spirit. How many of us have no self-control over things like eating, pornography, working all the time, time management, or a hobby? How many of us have no control over saying "no" to the things that will harm us? What a dilemma this is. But the Bible says self-control is a fruit of the Spirit which means one thing – you CAN have victory over these things.

Merriam Websters Collegiate Dictionary (10th Edition) defines self-control as:

"restraint exercised over one's impulses, emotions, or desires."

The Bible is filled with warnings against harmful activities. Lust produces things like adultery, pre-marital sex, and addictions to pornography. Anger produces violence. Dating non-Christians can end up in an unequally-yoked marriage. Ignoring your parent's godly advice can produce heartache for many years. All of us have impulses, emotions, and desires, and yet how can we exercise restraint? How do we walk by a computer that has pornography plastered all over it? How do we stop calling that person who isn't a Christian and we know is not right for us? How do we listen and obey our parents when everything they are telling us is not what we want to hear?

Self-control is tough, and we would venture to say that restraint cannot happen apart from the Holy Spirit working in our lives. We need godly people in our lives to be honest with and who can hold us accountable to the things we have no restraint over. We need to be continually in prayer over whatever our issue is. What we do know is that sometimes God takes some things away overnight. I (Rob) spent most of my life swearing, and when I became a Christian, God seemed to take that away from me immediately. But other things seem to take months or even years.

Some self-control issues take time and prayer, even fasting. If you can't seem to break a habit, try taking a day and stop eating. Whenever you get hungry, start praying for the ability to stop whatever you have a problem with. It is amazing what happens when you start praying all day. A fast could mean missing one meal, two meals, or not eating all day. Maybe it is a liquid-only fast or no chocolate chip cookies or ice cream. Whatever it takes in your life to feel some kind of discomfort that reminds you to pray could be a break-through in your life.

Sometimes as Christians we feel we can do things all on our own, that we don't need anyone's help. If you have a self-control issue, find someone who will pray with you and help you through it. If it is pornography, maybe you need to get rid of the computer. If it is a relationship that is bad, maybe you need to move to another part of the city. There are things we can and should do, and in the process, God will work to change us from the inside out.

1 Corinthians 9:25:

"Everyone who competes in the games exercises self-control in all things. They then do it to receive a perishable wreath, but we an imperishable."

Many people when they come to Christ assume it will be an easy ride, and that Jesus will make life so much easier than it is. This verse in Corinthians lets us know that Christians have to go into strict training - it might mean doing everything we can to stay away from things we have no self control over. It might mean we are in God's Word morning, noon and night so we can learn from God what He wants us to do. It might mean joining an accountability group. It might mean talking with your church and asking for help. Training is hard and takes a lot of work. Do whatever it takes to help yourself with the problem of self control.

We have a friend who shows horses. We asked her one night how many hours a day she spends riding and training her horses. She told us about eight hours, five to six days a week. Why would anyone do that? We would assume it is because she wants her horses to win. She wants her family to be the best and to take home the trophies. This is a great illustration of training ourselves in the things of God. In order to know Him and what He wants us to do with our lives, we have to train, spend time with Him, and spend the time to read His Word. Only then can He begin to change our self-control issues from the inside out.

1 Peter 3:8-9:

"To sum up, all of you be harmonious, sympathetic, brotherly, kindhearted, and humble in spirit; not returning evil for evil or insult for insult, but giving a blessing instead;

for you were called for the very purpose that you might inherit a blessing."

CHAPTER 16

FRUIT PRODUCED BY DISCIPLINE

Hebrews 12:11 "All discipline for the moment seems not to be joyful, but sorrowful; yet to those who have been trained by it, afterwards it yields the peaceful fruit of righteousness."

Most everyone we know, including ourselves, hates discipline, but we are sure our children hate it more! It is so hard to explain to them that when we discipline them, it is because we love them. The same is true with God. We are His children, and with that comes a responsibility on His part to correct us when we do something wrong.

This summer we were up at Lake Powell and we were saving a spot on a beach for some people we had invited. With boats and seadoos, we had surrounded the beach so others knew it was our territory (or our idol, as we soon discovered!). Most people know lake etiquette well enough to know not to park near an occupied campsite. We had left the kids at home trying to get a few days of "alone" time to try to finish this book. One evening we looked out to find about ten tents being set up on "our" beach. We were shocked to say the least, but then we were mad. Who could be this rude? Who would set up camp right in front of our boats? Who would do this to us?

When I (Rob) went to talk to them, I wasn't in a very fruitful mood. I told them not to use our firewood since we had been saving it for the people we invited. I found out it was a church camp filled with boys from a non-Christian religion which made the situation all the more frustrating. Then I left. We were annoyed every time we looked out the window, still amazed that someone would do this to us (we must have actually thought this beach was ours)!

The next morning, Lisa woke up and walked onto the front deck just in time to see me walking back from talking to the church group leader. Earlier as I read my Bible on the front deck and prayed my usual "search-me oh-God-and-know-my-heart" prayer, **(Psalm 139:23-24, "Search me, O God, and know my heart; try me and know my anxious thoughts; and see if there be any hurtful way in me, and lead me in the everlasting way")** the Lord impressed upon me that we were acting more like non-Christians than children of God. I went over to their tents, and apologized to the leader, and told him they were welcome to our firewood.

When I came back, I told Lisa that while I was looking out at the tents, I visualized Jesus walking up to these kids – not to yell at them for camping on our beach, but to share the gospel with them. Ouch. It was definitely a discipline moment. We both felt ashamed of ourselves and realized how selfish and self-centered we were. After confessing this as sin and making it right with the campers, we were able to have the "peaceful fruit of righteousness."

That is how God trains us. The beach we were on gave us more lessons than we care to remember. It is amazing when God wants to teach us something, how, if we don't learn it the first time, He will try again until we get it. Two weeks before we battled over this same stupid beach. We had our family with us and they were trying out their new houseboat as we tried to protect the beach from unwanted guests. Just after sundown, a small boat pulled in right beside us while we finished dinner, and I (Lisa) could do nothing but continue to complain about the lack of lake etiquette. My brother was with us and he said something that God used once again to discipline my rotten attitude. He said, "Let's get some food together and give them something to eat."

Ouch, once again. I couldn't believe my attitude was so pointed inward and self-focused that I hadn't even thought to offer these people food. After my brother gave them the extra food, they came to the front of our boat with their dog and their words were, "We thought you were going to kick us off your beach but instead you fed us. Thank you very much for dinner." And then they walked away.

Another discipline moment (we hate that beach), but what it taught us was that we needed to really ask God to give us a heart for people – lost people who need Jesus. We needed to quit thinking of ourselves and start looking at every situation, regardless if someone is intruding on our privacy, regardless if we are on vacation, and see it as an opportunity to share Christ. We couldn't very well do that after telling the church group not to use our firewood. We were an embarrassment to the cause of Christ and yet God used this time to make us see how little fruit we were producing.

Discipline for the moment feels awful, but what it produces is a fruit to do the right thing. When God disciplines us, remember it is for our own good. It is so we can move toward looking and acting more like Jesus. He doesn't make us feel bad to hurt us, but to help us. The same thing happens with our own kids. Hopefully, our discipline will help them act the right way in life just as our Father wants the same for us.

The life of David in the Old Testament is a perfect example of the discipline of God. God calls David a "man after His own heart." God gives amazing favor to David and yet one day when his soldiers go out to battle, David doesn't go (first mistake). He sees a beautiful woman bathing on the roof in plain sight of him and David had a choice: turn away, look away, walk away. Instead, he inquires and sends for her – Bathsheba, a gorgeous woman who David couldn't resist. Unfortunately for David, she is married. Somehow, because he was king, we guess those minor details didn't matter to David, and yet those minor details are very major details to the God of the universe. David sleeps with her, she gets pregnant, he ends up murdering her husband to cover his sin, and then he waits.

Fortunately for David, God sends him a great friend, Nathan. Nathan confronts David of his sin and David acknowledges what he has done and replies "I have sinned against the Lord." Psalm 51 is a heartfelt prayer of David for what he had done. He wanted to be clean before his great God.

Psalm 51 says:
> **"Be gracious to me, O God, according to Your loving-kindness; according to the greatness of Your compassion blot out my transgressions. Wash me thoroughly from my iniquity and cleanse me from my sin. For I know my transgressions, and my sin is ever before me. Against You, You only, I have sinned and done what is evil in Your sight, so that You are justified when You speak**

and blameless when You judge. Behold, I was brought forth in iniquity, and in sin my mother conceived me. Behold, You desire truth in the innermost being, and in the hidden part You will make me know wisdom. Purify me with hyssop, and I shall be clean; wash me, and I shall be whiter than snow. Make me to hear joy and gladness, let the bones which You have broken rejoice. Hide Your face from my sins and blot out all my iniquities. Create in me a clean heart, O God, and renew a steadfast spirit within me. Do not cast me away from Your presence and do not take Your Holy Spirit from me. Restore to me the joy of Your salvation and sustain me with a willing spirit. Then I will teach transgressors Your ways, and sinners will be converted to You. Deliver me from bloodguiltiness, O God, the God of my salvation; then my tongue will joyfully sing of Your righteousness. O Lord, open my lips, that my mouth may declare Your praise. For You do not delight in sacrifice, otherwise I would give it; you are not pleased with burnt offering. The sacrifices of God are a broken spirit; a broken and a contrite heart, O God, You will not despise. By Your favor do good to Zion; build the walls of Jerusalem. Then You will delight in righteous sacrifices, in burnt offering and whole burnt offering; then young bulls will be offered on Your altar.

Unfortunately for David, sin brings consequences, and these consequences were painful. God said the child Bathsheba bore him would die. The sword would never depart from the house of David. His son would rebel and do in broad daylight what David and Bathsheba did in secret. David's life from then on was in turmoil. He was forgiven, but the consequences lasted his lifetime.

Discipline. We hate that word and yet that is what God promises to those of us who decide our way is better than God's way; it is what happens when we willfully disregard God and His laws for our lives. We need to remember God puts His commandments there for our protection.

We couldn't help but think about how our lives are a reflection of our Father in heaven. As we left our children with another family to go on this trip, we kept thinking we hoped they were being good, helping out, acting kind and considerate. Why? Because how they acted was a reflection on us since we were their parents. The same is true with God. We are a reflection of Him.

CHAPTER 17

REPENTANCE IS A FRUIT

Matthew 3:8 "Therefore bear fruit in keeping with repentance;"

After our sordid little beach story, we thought this would be a good time to talk about repentance. The word "repent" means "to change one's mind and act on that change." This would mean we realize what we did was wrong, and then we don't do it again. Let's say we cheated on a test at school. Repentance would mean confessing this to the teacher and not cheating again. If we look at pornography, we would change our mind, recognizing that as a child of God this activity is unacceptable to God and not do it again. If we rudely tell people they can't use our firewood, we would apologize and not do that again. This can only be done through the power of the Holy Spirit living within us.

Jesus talked a lot about repentance. After giving our life to Christ, He asks us to repent and turn from the things that displease Him. The problem is that repentance usually causes some kind of sorrow. I hurt someone, I lied to someone, I caused someone pain, and the result I feel is sorrow. But the Bible says this sorrow is a good thing, for it is leads us to repentance.

2 Corinthians 7:9 " I now rejoice, not that you were made sorrowful, but that you were made sorrowful to the point of repentance; for you were made sorrowful according to the will of God, so that you might not suffer loss in anything through us."

The problem with being sorrowful is that a lot of times the sorrow comes from getting caught. If you are caught in adultery, you are sorrowful. If you are caught gossiping about someone, you are sorrowful. If you are caught stealing something, you are sorrowful. But true sorrow brings about repentance. True sorrow says we will never commit adultery again, never spend time gossiping again, and never steal again. True sorrow will always bring true repentance.

Romans 2:4 "Or do you think lightly of the riches of His kindness and tolerance and patience, not knowing that the kindness of God leads you to repentance?"

Another part to understanding repentance is truly recognizing who God is. Because of His death on the cross, Jesus was responsible for saving us and giving us the gift of salvation. This thought alone should lead us to repentance. His kindness and what He did for us should be what leads us to do the right thing.

It is amazing how easy it is to forget what He has done for us. As we were at Lake Powell this summer and looking at the spectacular canyon walls, I (Lisa) was thinking how amazing it was that the beauty around me didn't hold the same "wow" factor it did the first time I saw it. They just became red rocks. Our fear is that the same thing can happen as we grow in our relationship with Christ. The "wow" factor of salvation is replaced with just settling in. The fear of God and His hatred of sin are replaced by complacency.

We tend to forget that part of the Christian life is the act of repentance - turning away from the things that displease God. Once again, this is a fruit that the Holy Spirit produces in our lives. As we read His Word and are confronted with the truth of how a Christian is supposed to live, He gives us the power and ability to turn away from the things He asks us not to do. Remember, when we become Christians, we can walk away from the destructive habits and patterns that were formed when we were not Christians. Read your Bible, seek help from your church, and be in prayer. God promises to change your life from the inside out.

CHAPTER 18

THE FIRST STEP TO PRODUCING FRUIT...ABIDE

John 15:5:

"I am the vine, you are the branches. He who abides in Me, and I in him, bears much fruit; for without Me you can do nothing."

Have you ever thought about what the word "abide" really means? The Enhanced Strong's Lexicon says there are 120 times where the word "abide" is used in the Bible. It is translated 61 times as "abide," 16 times as "remain," 15 times as "dwell", 11 times as "continue," nine times as "tarry," three times as "endure," and five other times miscellaneously. This is how the word would be defined:

*Not to depart
*To continue to be present
*To be held, kept, continually
*To continue to be, not to perish, to last, endure

Abiding in Christ is a continual process. Because of the strong nature of this word, it seems that abiding cannot be done on one Sunday morning each week. In order to produce fruit in our lives, we have to make spending time abiding in Christ a top priority. How does that play out in our busy lives? We have always heard that you spend time with whatever is the most important thing to you. Could that be your work? Your hobby? Your sports? Your children? Your spouse? Could it be that your life is not producing the kind of fruit it should be because you are lacking the one true ingredient? Abide. Spend time alone with your Bible studying what God has to say about your life. Spend time praying. If we say we love Christ, then why would this not be our top priority in our life?

The world we live in demands our time to be spent on things that have no eternal value. We want bigger houses and fancier cars. We leave for work early and stay there later because somehow the world has told us that to get ahead in life, that is what we must do. But the Bible says in Matthew 22:37 -39,

"And He said to him, "You shall love the Lord your God with all your heart, and with all your soul, and with all your mind. This is the great and foremost commandment. The second is like it, 'You shall love your neighbor as yourself.'"

The most important thing to God is that you love Him the most. As you can see, to be a Christian is to live opposite of what the world teaches. Our relationship to Jesus has to be the first and foremost thing in our life. He made it clear that to follow Him means we have to give up our lives for Him and do His work here on earth. As a Christian, your work takes on a new meaning – you are there to build relationships so you can share Christ with your co-workers.

You are there to show your boss that, as a Christian, you work the hardest and have the most integrity. Are your kids on a sports team? Realize God has placed these parents and children on this particular team with you so you can be a light and hopefully have an opportunity to share Christ with them. What about your neighbors? As a Christian, you realize God has placed you in that particular neighborhood so you can be a "missionary" to them.

The problem with all of this is that we do not have the right perspective on life. There are planes to catch and bills to pay and football games and dance practice. There are Bible studies and youth groups and children needing to go to the doctor and dentist. Our lives are full. But, if we claim to be a Christian, are these valid reasons not to spend time with Him? If He is calling us to live contrary to this world, wouldn't we make the time to spend with Him? ***Abide. Cling to. Remain. Dwell. Continue.*** That is what He calls us to do in order to bear fruit and live out what He has called us to do. But how? How do we do that in this busy, crazy world? Read your Bible and pray. We will examine this in the next chapters.

CHAPTER 19

ABIDING THROUGH THE BIBLE

Here is the first thing we must do in order to abide in Christ: read the Bible. Let's start by looking at what the Bible says about how important God's Words should be in our life. Psalm 119 has so much wisdom in that chapter alone. Here are some verses that should help us see how important the Bible should be to us. As you read these verses ask yourself the question below the verse.

Psalm 119:11 (NIV):

"I have hidden your word in my heart that I might not sin against you."

Have you hidden the Bible in your heart so you know what sin is?

Psalm 119:16:

"I shall delight in Your statutes; I shall not forget Your word."

Do you delight yourself in what God has to say?

Psalm 119:25:

"My soul cleaves to the dust; revive me according to Your word."

Does the Bible revive you when you are down?

Psalm 119:42:

"So I will have an answer for him who reproaches me, for I trust in Your word."

Do you have an answer for those that challenge your faith?

Psalm 119:67:

"Before I was afflicted I went astray, but now I keep Your word."

Do you understand that, if you are truly a child of God, He will discipline you if you wander from Him?

Psalm 119:74:

"Those who fear You will be glad when they see me, because I have hoped in Your word."

Are people glad to see you because they know you are a believer and trust in God?

Psalm 119:101:

"I have restrained my feet from every evil way, that I may keep Your word."

Do you walk away from evil practices because you want to keep God's Word?

Psalm 119:105:

"Your word is a lamp to my feet and a light to my path."

Do you read God's Word so you know where to go and what to do with your life?

Psalm 119:114:

"You are my hiding place and my shield; I hope in Your word."

Do you have hope in your life because of what God tells you in His Word?

Psalm 119:133:

"Direct my steps by Your word, and let no iniquity have dominion over me."

Do you read God's Word so sin will not dominate your life?

Psalm 119:147:

"I rise before the dawning of the morning, and cry for help; I hope in Your word."

Is hearing from God so important to you that you wake up early to read it?

Psalm 119:148:

"My eyes are awake through the night watches, that I may meditate on Your word."

When you wake up in the middle of the night, do your thoughts turn to what God has to say in His Word?

Psalm 119:154:

> **"Plead my cause and redeem me; revive me according to Your word."**

When hard times come in your life, are you revived through reading your Bible knowing that God pleads your case for you?

Psalm 119:160:

> **"The entirety of Your word is truth, and every one of Your righteous judgments endures forever."**

Do you pick and choose what you want to believe in the Bible, or do you see the Bible as God's Word to you in its entirety?

Psalm 119:161:

> **"Princes persecute me without a cause, but my heart stands in awe of Your word."**

Does it matter to you what others think, or do you only care what God thinks?

Psalm 119:162:

> **"I rejoice at Your word as one who finds great treasure."**

Do you look at the Bible as a treasure or just as something you are "supposed" to read?

Psalm 119:169:

> **"Let my cry come before You, O Lord; Give me under standing according to Your word."**

Do you look at life through the eyes of God's Word or through the eyes of the world?

Psalm 119 alone teaches us how important reading God's Word is in our lives. If we are too busy to read the Bible each day then we might be too busy! Something has to change in life. Wake up a little earlier; go to bed a little later. We have no problem scheduling appointments for our hair, nails or golf games, but what about scheduling an appointment each day with the King of the Universe, the One who saved us and calls us His own? Maybe start out with 15 minutes a day, and you will be amazed how, eventually that won't be enough. We can't know someone if we don't take the time to spend with them. If God calls us to love Him first then something has to change in our lives so we can act on that love.

As we talk with people throughout the day, we are amazed at how many people do not know what the Bible says about different issues. Although they have problems in their marriages, they have never taken the time to see God's answer. Although they have problems at work or with someone who has hurt them deeply, they have never turned to the source that will help them. Many people who claim to be Christians have no idea how to obey God because they do not know His commands. Our fear is that complacency has invaded the lives of people who claim the name of Christ. Few are challenged to read their Bibles. Few are taught this is not an option, but our relationship with God demands it. Few are taught we are to read our Bibles not just once through in a lifetime, but everyday for the rest of your life. Why? Because the more you read and study, the more you will be able to deal with the problems that come up in your life. The more you read, the more you will be able to answer others who are hurting and questioning.

Here are two examples of issues that the world seems to throw at us all the time. The problem is that we have to defend these issues with people who are not Christians along with defending them to those who claim Jesus as their Lord and Savior. Why? Why would we have to argue with a believer over what the Bible has to say? We would have to say that a lack of knowledge, a lack of study, or a lack of abiding would be the reason. As you read what the Bible says about divorce and homosexuality, look at your own reaction and see if you are taking the Bible as your final authority in your life. The world will tell you that you are judgmental; God will tell you that this is His truth.

Divorce:

If you have become a Christian, and your spouse is not a believer, condemns your faith and is angry that you now want to go to church and read your Bible, what should you do? The world would tell you that you need to get a divorce, start all over; you just need to be happy. The world would tell you life is too short to be unhappy, your happiness is all that matters, and you could find a Christian spouse and live happily ever after. That is the world talking. What does the Bible say?

1 Corinthians 7:10-16:

"Now to the married I command, yet not I but the Lord: A wife is not to depart from her husband. But even if she does depart, let her remain unmarried or be reconciled to her husband. And a husband is not to divorce his wife. But to the rest I, not the Lord, say: If any brother has a wife who does not believe, and she is willing to live with him, let him not divorce her. And a woman who has a husband, who does not believe, if he is willing to live with her, let her not divorce him. For the unbelieving husband is sanctified by the wife, and the unbelieving wife is sanctified by the husband; otherwise your children would be unclean, but now they are holy. But if the unbeliever departs, let him

depart; a brother or a sister is not under bondage in such cases. But God has called us to peace. For how do you know, O wife, whether you will save your husband? Or how do you know, O husband, whether you will save your wife?"

Matthew 5:32:

> **"But I say to you that whoever divorces his wife for any reason except sexual immorality causes her to commit adultery; and whoever marries a woman who is divorced commits adultery."**

1 Peter 3:1-4:

> **"Wives, likewise, be submissive to your own husbands, that even if some do not obey the word, they, without a word, may be won by the conduct of their wives, when they observe your chaste conduct accompanied by fear. Do not let your adornment be merely outward—arranging the hair, wearing gold, or putting on fine apparel— rather let it be the hidden person of the heart, with the incorruptible beauty of a gentle and quiet spirit, which is very precious in the sight of God."**

The Bible says the opposite of what the world says, and instead of leaving, you are commanded to stay with your spouse. Why? Why would God not want you to be happy? God's plan is different: stay, be loving, show your gentleness, let Christ be shown by your actions. The reason for this? So you might win your spouse to Christ. You never know what God is up to. Many marriages have been saved and husbands or wives have come to know Christ because of the believing spouse. Sometimes it happens over a short period of time, sometimes it takes a lifetime. When you stand in front of God someday, He will only ask you to give an account of your life and whether or not you obeyed His commands. He will not ask about your spouse. He wants a loving obedient response from you.

God does give reasons for divorce, but Malachi 2:16 says He hates divorce. The **biblical** reasons would be only if your spouse has been unfaithful and committed adultery (sexual), or if your unbelieving spouse leaves you. That's it.

Those are the ground rules that God has given us, and if we say we are Christians, then it is up to us to obey. For some of you that means a tough life ahead of you. For some of you that means a lonely life. But God promises He will never give you more than you can handle. Surround yourself with godly friends who will encourage you biblically. Find a church that will give you good, solid biblical advice. Always check what you are being told against what the Bible says. The Bible is so simple. Read it and obey it. It won't take a lot of sessions with a counselor to tell you that. Ecclesiastes 12:13 says, **"The conclusion, when all has been heard, is: fear God and keep His commandments, because this applies to every person."**

As a side note, please know that God can restore and make beautiful a marriage that has been marred by an adulterous affair. Just because a spouse has been unfaithful does not mean that a marriage should break up. A true repentant heart on the part of the adulterer and a true forgiving heart on the part of the spouse can produce a wonderful, restored marriage. Just because an adulterous affair has happened in your marriage does not mean you have to get a divorce. God has a miraculous way of restoring something that once seemed hopeless.

As another side note, if there is physical abuse in your

marriage, please seek immediate help. Separation not divorce, for the purpose of getting help, would be advised. Once again, God can restore something that seems impossible.

Let's try another issue, homosexuality.

Many people have no idea what the Bible says about this subject. Churches allow their clergy to live homosexual lifestyles and teach God's Word, and the world, along with a lot of churches and denominations, just accept it. The world will tell us we are being judgmental or it is none of our business. We will be told we don't have the right to tell others how to run their lives. We have to have the knowledge of what God's Word says, not so we can judge the persons lifestyle, but so we can be honest and warn people of what the truth is. A person living in an unrepentant homosexual lifestyle has a salvation issue. **Regardless if the person is a pastor or a parishioner, the bottom line is they cannot be a Christian.** How can we say that? Because the Bible does. If the Bible is our final authority in our life, we cannot pick and choose what we want to take as truth. Can a person be saved out of that lifestyle? **<u>ABSOLUTELY</u>**. God promises He can change a person from the inside out. Our responsibility as believers is to know what the Bible has to say and take a stand. When salvation is at stake for a person's life, we need to take this very seriously.

As we were writing this, a major news station came on with a well known politician's son talking about this exact issue. It was interesting because he started quoting Bible verses like "do not judge lest you be judged" and brought up Bible stories about how Jesus was all about forgiving the woman caught in adultery. The problem was that he was picking and choosing verses and passages in the Bible to go along with his theology. Not once did he quote a verse that showed how God viewed homosexuality. This man kept telling people that Jesus was just about love and forgiveness. The problem is that you have to take the Bible in its full context which means checking the entire Bible from Genesis to Revelation on a particular subject, not just one verse. God is loving and forgiving, but He also has a pure hatred of sin and His wrath will be on those who do not come to His Son in repentance and faith. We did not hear this on the television that day.

It is important to know the entire Bible, and it is important to know the true God of the Bible. That takes work and that takes study.

Here is what the Bible says about this issue.

1 Corinthians 6:9-11:

> **"Do you not know that *the unrighteous will not inherit the kingdom of God?* Do not be deceived. Neither fornicators, nor idolaters, nor adulterers, *nor homosexuals*, nor sodomites, nor thieves, nor covetous, nor drunkards, nor revilers, nor extortioners will inherit the kingdom of God. And such were some of you. But you were washed, but you were sanctified, but you were justified in the name of the Lord Jesus and by the Spirit of our God." (Emphasis ours)**

Just as another side note: we tend to get hung up on homosexuality as being "worse" than all other lifestyles. Please note that if you live in a lifestyle that consists of adultery (having sex with someone other than your spouse), or if you have pre-marital sex as a normal way of life and you are not married, you, too, would fall into the same category. These are all lifestyles that are inconsistent with being a child of God.

Romans 1:26-27:

> **"For this reason God gave them up to vile passions. For even their women exchanged the natural use for what is against nature. Likewise also the men, leaving the natural use of the woman, burned in their lust for one another, men with men committing what is shameful, and receiving in themselves the penalty of their error which was due."**

Leviticus 18:22:

> **"You shall not lie with a male as with a woman. It is an abomination."**

1 Timothy 1:9-10:

> **"knowing this: that the law is not made for a righteous person, but for the lawless and insubordinate, for the ungodly and for sinners, for the unholy and profane, for murderers of fathers and murderers of mothers, for manslayers, for fornicators, for sodomites, for kidnappers, for liars, for perjurers, and if there is any other thing that is contrary to sound doctrine..."**

1 Thessalonians 4:3-8:

> **"For this is the will of God, your sanctification: that you should abstain from sexual immorality; that each of you should know how to possess his own vessel in sanctification and honor, not in passion of lust, like the Gentiles who do not know God; that no one should take advantage of and defraud his brother in this matter, because the Lord is the avenger of all such, as we also forewarned you and testified. For God did not call us to uncleanness, but**

in holiness. Therefore he who rejects this does not reject man, but God, who has also given us His Holy Spirit."

As you can see from these verses, God says a person cannot be a Christian and live in a continual unrepentant, homosexual lifestyle. When someone says to us that a pastor can live this way and be a Christian, our response is the Bible says that is not possible. As you can see from the verses in I Corinthians 6:9-11, God says such a person like that "will not inherit the kingdom of God." The most wonderful part of that verse is where it says, "and such WERE some of you." Such hope. Such grace. There is God's promise that a person **can** get out of this lifestyle. It sounds like these people lived like this until they came to a true saving knowledge of Jesus. When a person gives his life to Christ, everything changes. As the Holy Spirit works in a life, He is working out the things that displease Him. Evidently, homosexuality is an abomination to God and is so serious that God says those who live it won't spend eternity with Him.

The reason this is such an important issue is that, as Christians, it is our responsibility to tell people the truth. We were on the website of a large church and responded to an E-mail from a man who said he loved going to church at this particular church for the last eleven years because he was in a homosexual relationship and he felt comfortable at this church – nobody ever judged him for his lifestyle. We were so shocked we e-mailed him and told him what the truth of the Bible says – that unless he repented and turned his back on his lifestyle he would spend eternity separated from God. He was never told the truth that his lifestyle could send him straight to hell. That is our responsibility - ___Not to be judgmental, but to hopefully be used by God to open someone's eyes to the truth of God's Word.___ Once again, the world says it is not our business. The Bible says it is.

These are just two issues that we, as the body of Christ, have to deal with on a daily basis. We have to know how to respond. We have to know what God has to say about these things. That is why the Bible is so important. There are so many other issues the world would have a totally opposite view on: forgiveness, children, anger, bitterness, marriage, sex, living together before marriage, how to treat those who hurt you. The list could go on and on. It is our responsibility to learn God's Word and help those who are having these issues. We need Christians to take a stand and to tell the truth of what God has to say. In the end, the only thing that will matter is what God has to say, not our families, or friends, or the T.V., or talk radio. The Bible has to be our final authority, and it is up to us to take the time to read it and know it.

Psalm 1:1-3:

"Blessed is the man who walks not in the counsel of the ungodly, nor stands in the path of sinners, nor sits in the seat of the scornful; but his delight is in the law of the Lord, and in His law he meditates day and night. He shall be like a tree planted by the rivers of water, that brings forth its fruit in its season, whose leaf also shall not wither; and whatever he does shall prosper."

Webster's Dictionary defines the word "meditate" as follows:

1.) To reflect on: ponder, 2.) To plan or intend in the mind, to engage in contemplation.

The Bible says we need to meditate on His law day and night. To do this would mean a continual process starting with the minute you wake up. Our suggestion would be to wake up at least 30 minutes early each morning. Get your Bible out and start reading. Maybe you want to start in the New Testament and read three chapters a day until you are done. Maybe you want to read through the Bible in a year – there are Bibles that take you through this each day. Maybe you could read the chapter in Proverbs each day that corresponds with the date. (Proverbs has 31 chapters which could be easily read each day). Maybe you could read a small book in the Bible like 1 John or Philippians, and read it each day for a month. There are no set rules for reading the Bible except one. Just do it! You will be amazed at what you will learn. As you read, write a few things down that you have learned, things you can take with you during the day. Maybe there is a verse that touches your life for that day. Write it down and try to memorize it. Put it on your car mirror or on the refrigerator. Keep God's Word in front of you all day.

CHAPTER 20

ABIDING THROUGH PRAYER

The second part of abiding in Christ is through prayer. Check out these verses.

Acts 6:4:

> **"but we will give ourselves continually to prayer and to the ministry of the word."**

Colossians 1:9:

> **"For this reason we also, since the day we heard it, do not cease to pray for you, and to ask that you may be filled with the knowledge of His will in all wisdom and spiritual understanding;"**

1 Thessalonians 5:17:

> **"pray without ceasing,"**

Mark 1:35:

> **"Now in the morning, having risen a long while before daylight, He went out and departed to a solitary place; and there He prayed."**

Psalm 55:17:

"Evening and morning and at noon I will pray, and cry aloud, and He shall hear my voice."

Praying is another way of being attached to Christ. Prayer is just talking to God and being silent enough to listen. These verses show us something important: praying isn't just something we do when we are in trouble. Prayer isn't something we do to get something like a new car or good weather for our golf game. Prayer is communication with the God of the universe all day long. Evening, morning and noon sounds like an all day event. It would mean at work, on vacation, when things are good and when things are bad. That would mean thanking Him for the blessings He has given you such as your children, your job, and your health. It would mean praying for the trials in your life such as your children, your job, and your health. In all things God wants us to communicate with Him.

As you abide in Christ through prayer, you will be challenged by things like timing and unanswered prayer. Recognize that God's timing is usually completely different than our timing. He sees the big picture; He is working behind the scene. As we pray, we learn to pray as Jesus: "not my will but Your will be done." As we pray something happens to us; we change. What God wants for our lives suddenly seems more important than what we want.

Maybe you want a new house and yours doesn't sell, but maybe God knows you have a neighbor who needs to hear about Christ and He is leaving you there to share your faith. Maybe you have been sick and you want to get better, but maybe He is using your sickness as a tool to show others that His grace is sufficient even when your prayers seem to bounce off the ceiling. Maybe you have a child who is on drugs and on the streets, and you lay awake at night praying for his safety but maybe God is allowing him to go through this so that when he comes to Christ he will be able to help others who are on drugs and on the streets. Maybe your husband is not a Christian and he is a jerk to you and the kids, but maybe God wants to use you to help other women who are in the same situation.

The problem is we live in a world that is "all about me." As a Christian, our life has to be "all about Him" and His timing, His ways, His answer of "no," His answer of "wait." We pray, we wait and we don't walk away if we don't get what we want. We keep praying until God changes the situation or He changes us. Praying is not so much about getting what we want, but more about coming under His sovereign control and allowing Him to do with us what He thinks best. That is prayer. It is communication. It is letting God know what our wishes are but all along praying for what He deems best for our lives. Dating someone? Pray for what God wants, not for what you want. We have seen too many people make bad choices and live in misery all their lives. Want that job? Pray for what God wants. If it doesn't go through, rejoice. Want that new house? Pray for what God wants. If it sells out from underneath you, be glad. It might have been full of termites!

Start a prayer list, a list of people who you would like to pray for. If you have a lot of time to pray, then put everyone you can think of on it! That method can be overwhelming so you could make your list according to days.

- Monday would be set aside to pray for our immediate family, spouse, children, and grandchildren. Pray for the salvation of those not saved or any problems that your family is having.
- Tuesday would be to pray for other family members, parents, sisters, brothers, aunts, and uncles.

- Wednesday would be the day to pray for all your friends that are Christians. Pray that God would help them grow in their faith and for any other personal problems they might be having.
- Thursday would be the day to pray for all the people in your life that are not Christians. They could be family members, friends, neighbors, or co-workers. They could be students, teachers, or bosses! Anyone you have a burden for to come to Christ would be on this list. Pray that God would touch their lives and that you would have opportunities to share your faith with them. Pray that your life would be so different that they would see Christ in you.
- Friday pray for ministries that you know of such as the Crisis Pregnancy Center or Campus Crusade for Christ. Any ministry you are involved with or have a heart for, pray for them.
- Saturday pray for the government (the President, the senators, the public officials). Pray for your schools, the principals, and the teachers.
- Sunday would be the day to pray for your church, your pastor, and your elders. Pray for the service that day, that it would touch many lives.

Maybe this is too much of a regimented schedule and you are better at just praying throughout the day for things that come to your mind. Maybe you pray for people as you see them. Maybe you keep a list in your car and pray on your way to work. There are no set ways to do this; each person has a different schedule that works for them. The bottom line is that it doesn't matter how and where you pray, just as long as you do it!

Abiding in Christ is a daily, ongoing practice. The more we stay attached to Him, read His Word and pray and listen, the more we will get to know Him. To bear fruit, we must abide in Him.

CHAPTER 21

EXAMINE YOURSELF

2 Corinthians 13:5 – "Test yourselves to see if you are in the faith; examine yourselves! Or do you not recognize this about yourselves, that Jesus Christ is in you—unless indeed you fail the test?"

As we come to the last few chapters we want to challenge you to examine yourself. This is always the first step to examine your life and your belief system. Don't examine your friends or parents or co-workers or relatives; examine yourself. We need to look at our life and our faith and make sure that we are in the faith. What does that mean?

Did you come to a point in your life when you realized you were a sinner, truly separated from God because of that sin and did you put your faith and trust in Jesus alone to save you? Is your life changing because of that decision? Philippians 1:6 says, **"For I am confident of this very thing, that He who began a good work in you will perfect it until the day of Christ Jesus..."** This verse means that God has begun a work in you and your life will continue to change. He will be working out the sin in your life and replace it with fruit. Your life will never be the same again as you learn to love Him and trust Him completely.

This process takes time and work. Is this happening in your life? Are you reading your Bible, studying God's Word to see what He expects of you? Are you in a good Bible-teaching church each week that is helping you grow as a Christian? Do you have Christian friends or people that are helping you grow in your faith? Are you praying? Are you sharing your faith with people who need to know what it truly means to be a Christian?

In 1 Samuel 15:22 there is a scene where Saul completely dis-obeyed God and yet Saul used the excuse that his disobedience was okay because it was to make a sacrifice to God. Samuel said to him: **"Has the Lord as much delight in burnt offerings and sacrifices as in obeying the voice of the Lord? Behold, <u>to obey is better than sacrifice,</u> and to heed than the fat of rams.** (emphasis ours)"

Matthew 7:21 adds **"Not everyone who says to Me, 'Lord, Lord,' shall enter the kingdom of heaven, but he who <u>does the will of My Father</u> in heaven** (Emphasis ours)."

James 2:17-20 says, **"Even so faith, if it has no works, is dead, being by itself. But someone may well say, "You have faith and I have works; show me your faith without the works, and I will show you my faith by my works." You believe that God is one. You do well; the demons also believe, and shudder. But are you willing to recognize, you foolish fellow, <u>that faith without works is useless?</u>** (Emphasis ours)."

The Bible is clear: our obedience to God's Word also shows us if our faith is true or not. Please remember that we are not and will never be perfect. Someone told us once that being a Christian is like being an onion – God is peeling away the old things that displease Him one layer at a time. If you are a Christian then as you read the Bible the Holy Spirit will impress upon your heart the things that displease Him and you will need to turn your back on them.

The problem we face so often is the idea that you can live any way you want and God will just look the other way. So many people use the grace of God to live unholy lives and yet feel they are under the "grace" umbrella. Is that truly what the Bible says? Look at what Romans 6:1-2 says,

"What shall we say then? Are we to continue in sin so that grace may increase? May it never be! How shall we who died to sin still live in it?"

If you have been taught all your life that it doesn't matter what you do or how you act, we ask you to see if that is really what God's Word says. If you truly are a Christian you do not have a license to sin and do what you want. There is a commercial on television that advertises for the city of Las Vegas. In it the people are clearly doing things they aren't supposed to and yet the slogan at the end is "What happens here stays here." When you become a Christian the opposite actually happens. When you understand the grace and for-giveness of God and that the blood of Jesus on the cross takes your place so you can spend eternity with Him forever – that produces gratitude. It also produces a hatred of sin, a realization that you have a new life and you don't want to live like you used to. 1 Corinthians 6:9-11 says,

"Or do you not know that the unrighteous will not inherit the kingdom of God? Do not be deceived; neither fornicators,

nor idolaters, nor adulterers, nor effeminate, nor homosexuals, nor thieves, nor the covetous, nor drunkards, nor revilers, nor swindlers, will inherit the kingdom of God. Such were some of you; but you were washed, but you were sanctified, but you were justified in the name of the Lord Jesus Christ and in the Spirit of our God."

This verse says there has to be a life change – we cannot do what we used to do. It says such "were" some of us indicating a lifestyle change that happened when we became a Christian. Sometimes these changes take place overnight; most of the time these changes take place over time.

Look at what Romans 8:29-30 has to say; **"For those whom He foreknew, He also predestined to become conformed to the image of His Son, so that He would be the firstborn among many brethren; and these whom He predestined, He also called; and these whom He called, He also justified; and these whom He justified, He also glorified."**

The purpose for becoming a Christian is to spend our life conforming to the image of Jesus. Our lives take on a different meaning and a different purpose. Remember, we cannot take one verse and base our whole belief system on that. We have to let Scripture interpret Scripture. Check out these other verses:

Philippians 1:21:
"For to me, to live is Christ, and to die is gain."

Can you say this about yourself?

Philippians 2:12:

"So then, my beloved, just as you have always obeyed, not as in my presence only, but now much more in my absence, work out your salvation with fear and trembling;"

Do you work out your salvation with fear and trembling, taking your faith as something very serious?

Philippians 3:7-10:

"But whatever things were gain to me, those things I have counted as loss for the sake of Christ. More than that, I count all things to be loss in view of the surpassing value of knowing Christ Jesus my Lord, for whom I have suffered the loss of all things, and count them but rubbish so that I may gain Christ, and may be found in Him, not having a righteousness of my own derived from the Law, but that which is through faith in Christ, the righteousness which comes from God on the basis of faith, that I may know Him and the power of His resurrection and the fellowship of His sufferings, being conformed to His death;"

Do you look at the things you have accomplished in your life as rubbish compared to the knowledge of knowing Christ?

Acts 4:13:

"Now as they observed the confidence of Peter and John and understood that they were uneducated and untrained men, they were amazed, and began to recognize them as having been with Jesus."

Can people tell by your lifestyle that you are a Christian?

Acts 4:20:

"for we cannot stop speaking about what we have seen and heard."

Because of what Christ has done for you, do you feel the need and urgency to tell others?

Matthew 10:32:

"Therefore everyone who confesses Me before men, I will also confess him before My Father who is in heaven."

Are you afraid to tell others you are a Christian?

Matthew 10:38:

"And he who does not take his cross and follow after Me is not worthy of Me."

Jesus demanded a total commitment, one which led (and did for many) to death for following Him. Do you have that kind of commitment?

The point to this whole section is to make sure you are truly a believer. Not a follower of the shallow, easy-belief system, but a true follower of Jesus, one who has given his whole life, one who understands the cost of being a true disciple of Christ.

A couple years ago Asia was hit with one of the largest tsunami's in history in which the death toll was over 100,000. The destruction included nine Mission of Mercy centers in Sri Lanka where children were being taught about Jesus. Do you think the missionaries who worked in these centers understood the cost of following Jesus? This was not just some minor decision they made to ask Jesus in their hearts. This was a life-long commitment to share Jesus with children and because of their faith and obedience there will be many in heaven because they counted the cost.

We are not saying everyone should go and be missionaries in a foreign country – God calls some Christians to do that, but He calls the rest of us to be missionaries in our neighborhoods, at our schools, at our work, at our homes, to our families, and to our friends. We do not have to go to the mission field to do that!

Examine yourself – see what kind of fruit is being produced in your life. True Christians understand what it means to follow Jesus, and because of that, their lives produce true fruit.

CHAPTER 22

WHAT SOIL ARE YOU?

We thought this would be a good chapter to end this book. What is your life producing? If honestly asked what type of soil you are, what would you say? Please examine these four scenarios and look at your own life.

It seems when Jesus was telling the parable of the soils in Mark 4, He wanted us to realize what a true conversion was versus what a false conversion was. Most of us have friends, family, or neighbors that would readily tell us they are Christians, but Jesus explains to us that there are those who claim to be saved and yet only one out of the four seeds is truly His. How can we tell? Fruit. Jesus tells us that the person whose life produces fruit is the person that is a Christian. Let's examine this parable of the four soils to see where you are in your life

Mark 4:13 -20 says,
   "And He said to them, "Do you not understand this parable? How then will you understand all the parables? The sower sows the word. And these are the ones by the

wayside where the word is sown. When they hear, Satan comes immediately and takes away the word that was sown in their hearts. These likewise are the ones sown on stony ground who, when they hear the word, immediately receive it with gladness; and they have no root in themselves, and so endure only for a time. Afterward, when tribulation or persecution arises for the word's sake, immediately they stumble. Now these are the ones sown among thorns; they are the ones who hear the word, and the cares of this world, the deceitfulness of riches, and the desires for other things entering in choke the word, and it becomes unfruitful. But these are the ones sown on good ground, those who hear the word, accept it, and bear fruit: some thirtyfold, some sixty, and some a hundred."

The sower would represent someone who shares the gospel or "the seed" with another person. If you were going to tell someone about Christ, then you would spend the time to explain sin and how it separates a person from God. You would tell them that Jesus is the only way to God, that He bridges the gap between a holy God and a sinful man. You would let them know that a decision to follow Christ means repentance of the things that offend Him. They would need to know that this is a free gift from God, that Jesus came to take away their sin and give them eternal life. It is a free gift, but it will cost them their lives; it will cost them everything. Out of a grateful heart for what Christ did on the cross for them, their lives will change, love Him, and want to serve Him. A clear presentation of the gospel would be the seed that you, the sower, would be sharing with another person.

The problem is that many are sowing a false seed, one that

promises heaven without any true commitment, wealth and prosperity if you give more money, and health if you have enough faith. None of these things are true. God has never promised heaven to anyone who has not fully committed his life to Jesus as the "Lord" (which means ruler) of his life. God has never promised wealth if you give more money. He does promise that you will be blessed, but that could mean spiritual blessings (people coming to know the Lord through you) rather than financial blessings. He never promises health, He does promise that "His grace is sufficient for you" in times when you are not as healthy as you would like.

It all comes down to a matter of the heart. Are you giving money to get more money, or are you giving to help further the Kingdom of God? Do you care about missions or other ministries that are out sharing Christ? Do you embrace and realize your money is what God will use to make this possible? Giving is a far more important matter than just putting money in the church offering in hopes that God will make you rich.

Health is another thing people are being offered if they just have enough "faith" to believe. When Paul had a "thorn is the flesh," he begged God three times to take it from him, and yet God said no. Do you think the man who penned "For me to live is Christ and to die is gain" didn't have enough faith? Does God heal? Absolutely. Does He heal all people who pray and have faith? Absolutely not! God heals those He wants to for His purposes so He can get the glory. We knew a thirteen year old boy who had cancer and was baptized in our pool a few years ago. We prayed and prayed and prayed for God to heal him, and yet God's answer was "no". We have no idea why God would say "no" to our prayer, but we know it wasn't because we didn't have enough faith. We KNEW God could heal him if He wanted, and yet we had to come to terms with the fact that God is sovereign and in control and He does what He thinks is best. We need to remember as we close our prayers the little addition that is in the Lord's Prayer, "Thy kingdom come, YOUR will be done." We need to pray and yet have enough faith that if the answer is no, no is an okay answer.

Now let's look at the four responses to the seeds being sown. The first seed thrown beside the road represents those that want nothing to do with the gospel. It could be offensive to them, or it could be they are happy with their life and don't want it to be interrupted with some "religion." We all have people in our lives like this. We try to tell them about Jesus, and they look at us like we are some kind of freak. They are completely unresponsive and hard hearted about any thought of God. Because of their hard heart, it is easy for Satan to come and snatch the seed away. **Romans 1:20** says:

**"For since the creation of the world His invisible attributes
are clearly seen, being understood by the things
that are made, even His eternal power and Godhead, so
that they are without excuse,.."**

These people have no excuse, the Bible says that creation alone "screams" the existence of God and yet they refuse to believe.

The second seed is thrown upon a rocky soil, soil which has a little dirt on top but rocks underneath. This person is one who hears the gospel and is so excited! They think that the youth group is so much fun, camp was a blast, church and concerts are great fun, but because they had not taken the time to study or learn God's Word, they have no depth or root and they walk away. You may know many people like this. You take them to church, they raise their hand to accept Christ, they are excited for a few months but when problems or trouble come, they walk away. Suddenly, they don't think being a Christian is much fun anymore. Nobody told them that trials and hardship should be expected. Nobody told them that God wanted to change them and make them look more like His Son Jesus.

Maybe this person lost his job, maybe he got sick, maybe his kids rebelled but he couldn't put together that bad things happen to Christians, so he walked away, never really understanding what a true commitment to Christ really meant.

The third seed is representative of what our life was like most of the time. We went to church and thought we were fine, but what we found out was that the things of the world were more important to us than the things of God. This is a tough group to recognize because, just like us, you don't see these people walk away from God. This is the seed that has been thrown among the thorns; the world chokes out any true understanding of what it means to follow Christ. This person has possibly "accepted Christ," but, once again, never understands what that means. This group sits on the fence on Sunday morning but the truth of what it truly means to be a Christian never penetrates their heart or their life.

The fourth soil represents those that are true Christians. They do not have hard hearts, they have soft, pliable hearts with a desire to know God and grow in Him. They abide in Him since that is the only way true fruit is produced. They read His Word and they allow the Holy Spirit to work on and change their lives. This seed produces fruit in some more than others, but they all produce actions and attitudes that prove they are Christians.

If you look at the soils represented here and see that your life is more like the first, second or third soil, we ask you to truly give your life to Jesus. Examine yourself and see if your relationship with God through Jesus is a true conversion. If not, by prayer we ask that you cry out to Him in repentance and faith.

So the question would be, "which soil are you?" Has God's Word penetrated your life and soul so that you are producing fruit? Can you see a true difference from one year to the next? Hopefully, as you examine your life, the answer to the question "Got Fruit?" will be a resounding "Yes!"

If you have any questions or comments, please e-mail us at:

lisalaizure@aol.com
or
robslaizure@aol.com

Visit us at our website:
www.dollarchristianbooks.com